# On the Mall

# ON THE MALL

*Presenting
Maroon Tradition-Bearers
at the 1992 FAF*

Richard & Sally Price

Special Publications of the Folklore Institute No. 4
*Indiana University*
BLOOMINGTON

Richard and Sally Price have been learning and writing about
Afro-Caribbean life since the early 1960s. They now spend each
fall semester in Virginia, at the College of William & Mary
(where RP is Professor of Anthropology and History and SP is
Professor of Anthropology and American Studies) and the rest of
the year in rural Martinique.

ISBN: 1-879407-06-X paper edition; 1-879407-07-8 cloth edition
Distributed by Indiana University Press,
Bloomington and Indianapolis

Printed in the United States of America

# Contents

Human displays teetertotter on a kind of semiotic seesaw, equipoised between the animate and inanimate, the living and the dead. The semiotic complexity of exhibits of people, particularly those of an ethnographic character, may be seen in reciprocities between exhibiting the dead as if they are alive and the living as if they are dead, reciprocities that hold as well for the art of the undertaker as they do for the art of the museum preparator. Ethnographic displays are part of a larger history of human display, in which the themes of death, dissection, torture, and martyrdom are intermingled.

(Kirshenblatt-Gimblett 1991:398)

# Preface

> Ethnographic truths are thus inherently *partial*—commit-
> ted and incomplete. . . . But once accepted and built into
> ethnographic art, a rigorous sense of partiality can be a
> source of representational tact.
>
> (Clifford 1986:7)

What follows is an intimate account of a brief, exhilarating, and often
unsettling experience: our participation in the 1992 Festival of American Folklife (FAF) as "presenters"—cultural mediators between African
American Maroons from Suriname and French Guiana and the festival-
goers who came to see them.

Trained as anthropologists, for the past three decades we have
been involved with Afro-Caribbean peoples, particularly the Maroons
(descendants of escaped slaves) of the Suriname rainforest. Throughout,
aspects of life that tend to interest folklorists—play languages, children's
games, popular songs, tale-telling, the graphic arts, material culture,
music, and dance—have figured prominently in our ethnographic
fieldwork. These topics have also held an important place in our
teaching and writing: either together or separately, we've taught courses
on Afro-American folklore at Yale, Johns Hopkins, and Stanford, published articles on a variety of "folkloric" subjects, and written a book
centered on transcriptions/translations of Maroon folktales. RP's work
on oral history has been read partly in conjunction with this orientation; his *First-Time* (1983) won the annual book prize of the American
Folklore Society. And for the past two years, we have been engaged in
research on the public exhibition of culture, particularly in museums,
drawing on material from three continents. It was very much in the
context of all these involvements that we became "participant observ-
ers" at the FAF.[1]

Each year's Festival is an enormously complex enterprise; we are
aware that our own experience touched on only a small part of the
whole. Despite its preponderance in the world of American public

folklore, there is surprisingly little written about the FAF by analysts outside the Smithsonian (see Siporin 1992), and there has been "little, if any, critical attention . . . from the perspective of the participants themselves" (Bauman et al. 1992:2). Fortunately, during the past year, all this has begun to change (see, in particular, Bauman et al. 1992 and Cantwell 1993). We hope that our own observations, limited though they are, may contribute constructively to the ongoing rethinking, within the Smithsonian and beyond, about the workings of the FAF and cognate cultural representations.

Bauman, Sawin, and Carpenter, who wrote the first systematic study of the Festival, recognized that much of what they were putting in print had already existed in the form of generalized experience for some years, commenting that "anyone who has worked in a festival will find much of our data familiar" (1992:4). In similar fashion, the experiences and reflections in our own account are surely not unique. One pre-publication reader of this essay, long familiar with the FAF, wrote that "it absolutely comports with the reports, stories, tales, and other communications that circulate at the FAF while it's underway, such things as I've heard again and again, but always in a form very little above the level of gossip." Because observations on the Festival have so rarely been written down, and because our own reactions to it are situated within larger discussions about the ethics of anthropological/folkloric enterprises in the 1990s, we hope they may play a constructive role in the Festival organizers' longstanding efforts to learn from the past in making each year's event more rewarding than the last, for participants and visitors alike.

Richard Kurin, director of the Smithsonian's Center for Folklife Programs and Cultural Studies (which produces the Festival and has played such an important role in redirecting the Smithsonian as a whole in a more progressive, populist, and multicultural direction), has written that the FAF "is both a vehicle as well as an indicator of an open national cultural conversation" (1989:21). It is with our eyes wide open to the necessary partiality of our account that we accept his implied invitation to add new voices to that discussion. It should be clear to every reader that our view of the FAF is perspectival, and ours alone. Indeed, it is offered in the generous spirit of pluralism that pervades the FAF itself: another voice among the many that have something to say about this quintessentially American institution.

We are deeply grateful to Roger Abrahams, Kenneth Bilby, Robert Cantwell, and Edmund O'Reilly for comments that have allowed us to make this essay better. We also sent near-final drafts of the manuscript to Richard Kurin, who did not send us comments, and to Peter Seitel and Diana N'Diaye, who replied but asked us not to quote from their letters. We wish to thank the Smithsonian Institution Center for Folklife Programs and Cultural Studies for giving us access to internal reports about the 1992 FAF as well as audio tapes and photos of portions of the event. Thanks also to Rebecca Bateman, Roland L. Freeman, Shelby Givens, and Natalie Murray who provided additional photos.

This work forms part of a larger project about cultural representations that has been funded by the National Endowment for the Humanities, the John Simon Guggenheim Foundation, and the Wenner-Gren Foundation for Anthropological Research, to all of which we express our sincere gratitude.

*Anse Chaudière, May 1994*

# Exhibiting Others

And the Smithsonian—who would deny it?—has also
survived by juggling so-called science and so-called
entertainment.
                                                    (Boon 1991:259)

During the past fifteen years, anthropology's self-examination has laid
bare a side of its history that had previously been known only to
specialists—the role of the discipline's leaders, during the decades
surrounding the turn of the last century, in promoting the public
exhibition of "natives" for the enlightenment and entertainment of
European and American audiences. Although Columbus brought back
a half-dozen Caribbean "Indians" on his first voyage, ten Hurons
kidnapped by Jacques Cartier were presented to the court of François I
in 1536, a group of Eskimos were displayed as living rarities in Bristol in
1577, and the crowd costumed as "savages" at the *divertissement indien*
staged for Henri II in 1550 included some fifty Brazilian Tupinambas, it
was only in the second half of the nineteenth century that the Western
vogue for exhibiting exotic peoples became fully institutionalized,
with the wedding of anthropological science and show business.[2]

The first such U.S. exhibition, organized by Phineas T. Barnum in
1853 and also responsible for introducing the recently-invented sewing machine to New York, presented "the Wild Man of Borneo, Fijian
man-eaters . . . and an encampment of three hundred Indians from
fifty tribes" (Hinsley 1991:345).

> But the practice of dispatching agents to remote regions for the sole
> purpose of bringing back groups of exotic types for public display and
> private profit seems to have originated in the late 1870s with Hamburg
> animal trainer and zoo master Carl Hagenbeck. Sometime around 1876
> Hagenbeck hired Johan Adrian Jacobsen to bring a collection of artifacts
> and a Greenland Eskimo family of six to Hamburg, then travel with them
> through Europe for eight months. (ibid.; see also Corbey 1993:345–46,
> Faber and Wachlin 1990)

Prince Roland Bonaparte, inspired by his visit to the native villages at the 1883 colonial exposition in Amsterdam, caught the spirit of the age when he laid plans for what would become the even more ambitious Paris exposition of 1889:

> A universal exposition of the diverse populations of the globe, where all ethnic groups would be represented. It would be of the greatest interest also to present all the objects of daily life to which these populations are accustomed: inhabited villages with houses decorated and furnished as they are in the countries from which they have been brought, cooking done in the indigenous ways, etc. etc.—in a word, one would see people living their lives exactly as if one were to travel to the regions in which they live. (Bonaparte 1884:vi)

By this time, the Jardin Zoologique d'Acclimatation—the Paris zoo—had made a regular practice of exhibiting exotic peoples, along with its animals, during the summer months:

> Between 1877 and 1903, more than twenty groups from various countries were brought to the Jardin to be exhibited. In the summer, they were set up in a kind of replica of an indigenous village on the great lawn. . . . The roll call: 1877: Nubians, Eskimos; 1878: Gauchos, Russian Lapps; 1879: Nubians; 1881: Tierra del Fuegans; 1882: Galibis; 1883: Sinhalese, Araucanians, Kalmuks, "Redskins"; 1886: Sinhalese; 1887: Ashantis; 1888: Hottentots, Circassian Cossacks; 1890: Norwegian Lapps, Somalis; 1891: Dahomeans; 1892: Caribs; 1893: Paï-Pl-Bris [?]; 1899: Whirling Dervishes; 1902: Malabars; 1903: Ashantis. (Collomb 1992b:17–18)

The British (like the Portuguese, Germans, and Dutch) also adopted this exhibition genre with enthusiasm. In 1853, in a very popular Hyde Park African display, thirteen Kaffirs

> portrayed "the whole drama of Caffre life" against a series of scenes painted by Charles Marshall. They ate meals with enormous spoons, held a conference with a "witchfinder" . . . and enacted a wedding, a hunt, and a military expedition, "all with characteristic dances." (Altick 1978:282, cited in Kirshenblatt-Gimblett 1991:405)

In 1886, at the Colonial and Indian Exhibition in London, there was a compound just outside the exhibition buildings that housed

> Hindus, Muhammadens, Buddhists, Red Indians from British Guiana, Cypriotes, Malays, Kaffirs and Bushmen from the Cape and the inhabitants of Perak and Hong Kong. Their Queen Empress has taken a deep

interest in their welfare and parties of them have on two occasions visited Her Majesty—once at Windsor and once at Osborne. (*Reminiscences of the Colonial and Indian Exhibition* 1886:5, cited in Benedict 1983:46)

The European penchant for exhibiting the Other was not restricted to those chosen for the purpose: visitors, including scholars, from such "exotic" places as Egypt were also subjected to this special gaze:

> As Europe consolidated its colonial power, non-European visitors found themselves continually being placed on exhibit or made the careful object of European curiosity. The degradation they were made to suffer seemed as necessary to these spectacles as the scaffolded facades or the curious crowds of onlookers. The facades, the onlookers, and the degradation seemed all to belong to the organizing of an exhibit, to a particular European concern with rendering the world up to be viewed. (Mitchell 1992:292)

The American variant of these European events was usually connected to the large international expositions that dotted the United States between 1876 and the early twentieth century:

> For each of these expositions, Congress appropriated funds. . . . [and] continuing involvement of experts from the Smithsonian Institution in providing exhibits, advice, and display classifications also confirmed the intermeshing of upper-class purpose and federal power. . . . Anthropological attractions—consisting of cultural artifacts, lay-figure groupings of "primitive types," and selected nonwhites living in ethnological villages along the midways—charted a course of racial progress toward an image of utopia that was reflected in the main exposition buildings. (Rydell 1984:235)[3]

Frederick Ward Putnam, curator of the Peabody Museum at Harvard and head of the Department of Ethnology and Archaeology for the 1893 Chicago Columbian Exposition, boasted in an 1891 speech:

> The part of the ethnological exhibit, however, which will prove of the greatest popular interest and at the same time be regarded as an essential and appropriate display, will be the out-of-doors exhibit of the native peoples of America, in their own houses, dressed in their native costumes and surrounded by their own utensils, implements, weapons, and the results of their own handiwork. (cited in Hinsley 1991:347)

And indeed once the exhibit opened,

> A few yards north of the model [archaeological] ruins stood the outdoor ethnographic exhibits, notably Boas's group of Kwakiutl Indians from Fort

Rupert, British Columbia. Working through George Hunt, his informant among the Kwakiutl, Boas had brought fourteen individuals to Chicago. To add to the authenticity a village from Skidegate, on the Queen Charlotte Islands, was disassembled, complete with doorposts, and brought as well. In these environs, Boas intended, the Kwakiutl would perform various ceremonials and live as normally as possible. They slept on the floor in the Stock Pavilion. (ibid.:349)

As Rydell has written, "The net result [of the Chicago 1893 exhibitions] was an alliance between entertainment and anthropology replicated in subsequent fairs" (1984:63), and when former Smithsonian anthropologist W J McGee agreed to become head of the Anthropology Department for the St. Louis exposition of 1904, it was after having received assurances from the management that "anthropology [would be] the heart of their fair," and that he could "incorporate wide-ranging living ethnological displays under the direct supervision of anthropologists" (1984:162). Thus, the St. Louis exposition outdid Chicago in the scale of its "primitive" exhibits, displaying (besides American Indians, Pygmies, Patagonians, Ainus, and other exotic peoples) nearly twelve hundred Filipinos living in villages on a forty-seven acre site (Rydell 1984:167). And at the Seattle fair of 1909,

Following the precedent established by the University of Chicago at the Saint Louis fair, [the administrators of the University of Washington] invited noted Cambridge anthropologist Alfred C. Haddon to offer a summer-school course in conjunction with the exposition.... Haddon proved to be an invaluable asset to the exposition promoters. His course, "The Growth of Cultural Evolution around the Pacific," sanctioned the exposition as an educational undertaking, while his endorsement of the Igorot Village helped the concessionaires and exposition officials refute the charges made by a group of visiting Filipino sailors that the attraction was "indecent." (Rydell 1984:199)

But these American expositions, with their ethnological agendas of demonstrating the Ascent of Civilized Man and their Federal agendas of justifying recent American "conquests" (in the Philippines as well as over Native American groups), were only one of the venues for mutual support between anthropologists on the one hand and businessmen and government on the other. Another was the immensely popular "Ethnological Congress of Strange and Savage People" (sometimes called "The Grand Congress of Nations") that, between 1884 and 1896, formed part of the "Museum Department" of the Barnum & Bailey Circus (Monsanto 1992). In the public ideology of these extravaganzas, education and entertainment were constantly paired.

The program book for the 1894 Barnum & Bailey Greatest Show on Earth (Madison Square Garden) took pains to point out that this was

> not a senseless, meaningless display of old circus material . . . but an earnest and intelligent effort to *instruct the minds of all classes*, by showing them the many things they may previously have read about, but never saw before in their lives, and probably never would see if not provided for them by the manager of this show. (cited in Monsanto 1992:10, original italics)

Barnum & Bailey advertisements listed as participants in this Grand Congress:

> Bestial Australian Cannibals; Mysterious Aztecs; Embruited Big-Lipped Botocudoes; Wild Moslem Nubians; Ferocious Zulus; Buddhist Monks; Invincible Afghans; Pagan Burmese Priests; Ishmaelitish Todars; Dusky Idolatrous Hindus; Sinuous Nautch Girls; Annamite Dwarfs; Haughty Syrians; Oriental Giants; Herculean Japanese; Kaffres; Arabs; Persians; Kurds; Ethiopians; Circassians; Polynesians; Tasmanians; Tartars; Patans; Etc. (Monsanto 1992:16)[4]

In 1882, Spencer Baird, Director of the Smithsonian Institution, put his personal seal on this Ethnological Congress (which was later "eagerly attended" by members of the New York Ethnological Society), writing that it held "the highest interest in an anthropological point of view" (letter of recommendation for Barnum to use in his negotiations with foreign governments, cited in Monsanto 1992:17).[5]

With the gift of hindsight, scholars have at last begun to historicize past anthropological complicity in exhibiting "our" "others" (e.g., Benedict 1983, Corbey 1993, Hinsley 1991, Mitchell 1992, and Stocking 1987, 1992). Nevertheless, from a presentist perspective, it is difficult not to feel outrage, or at the very least sadness, at these spectacles. The dust jacket banner on *Ota Benga: The Pygmy in the Zoo* (Bradford and Blume 1992) may be sensationalist in proclaiming "One Man's Degradation in Turn-of-the-Century America," but the tale it spins is genuinely harrowing. A more dignified moral statement on Victorian-era exhibitionary practice is made by the starkly beautiful brochure *Kaliña*, which juxtaposes the haunting "anthropological" photos of Amerindians exhibited at the Paris zoo in 1892 with the words of their modern-day descendants, who still preserve a memory of their experience:

> They went away to the land of the whites. They were taken away by the whites in a great ship. The older sister of my mother went, with her brother and her father-in-law. . . . My mother told me all of this. . . .
>
> They were set up in a large house, with their drums. They had necklaces, feathered headdresses, dance rattles. . . . They were set up there. . . . They danced all day long. . . . Beginning in the morning the Kaliña danced, and the whites gathered to see them. There were many, very many. . . .
>
> They arrived in the land of the whites. The sister of my grandmother, Mariana, was also on the trip. . . .
>
> The whites had brought the Indians there to make money off of them. . . . The Kaliña danced all the time. . . . Later, the Kaliña fell ill because it was cold. . . . They began to cough. . . .
>
> Because of the cold, the whites had constructed a shelter in which they put the Kaliña, and they kept dancing, always dancing. . . . I don't know how long they stayed—maybe a month, maybe more—my mother didn't tell me that. After they'd fallen sick, the Kaliña stopped dancing, they simply couldn't go on. . . .
>
> So, they stayed there. Even though they had been ready to come home. . . . Some of them were taken to the hospital. . . . One of my mother's brothers was among those. . . . Only one of his sisters and his father-in-law made it back here. . . . On the eve of her departure, his sister went to see him in the hospital. He said to her, "Give me a little water, I'm dying of thirst.". . . She left him in the hospital. After that, his mother never heard another word about him. She never knew if he was alive or if he was dead.
>
> So, they came home. . . . But many hadn't survived. I don't know how many died. . . .
>
> When my mother would tell me this, she couldn't keep herself from crying, because of the brother who'd stayed behind there. She would cry as if all this had just happened. (Recorded in Langamankondre, Suriname, August 1991, cited in Collomb 1992a)

Fig. 1 *(On the adjacent page)* Six of the Kaliñas exhibited in Paris in 1892, photographed by Prince Roland Bonaparte. Reprinted from Collomb 1992a.

# Homing in on the FAF

The ideological wellsprings of the Festival of American Folklife, which began in 1967, are deep and dispersed.[6] Richard Kurin, director of the Smithsonian's Center for Folklife Programs and Cultural Studies, offers a particularly clear statement of purpose:

> The Festival of American Folklife, from its inception, has been conceived as part of a cultural conservation strategy for the National Museum. Underlying that strategy is the belief in cultural equity, cultural relativity and cultural pluralism—the belief that all cultures have something to say and a right to be heard, that questions of cultural superiority are moot, and that a world, nation and community with many cultures are enriched by that diversity. . . .
> *We do the Festival so that people can be heard.* . . .
> *We do the Festival so that practitioners may be encouraged to pass on their skills and knowledge.* . . .
> *The Festival contributes to the development of scholarship and museology.* . . .
> *The Festival symbolizes aspects of our own nation and sense of community.* (1989:12–19, original italics)

Peter Seitel, then director of the Smithsonian's Office of Folklife, stressed that the FAF was at once a theme park and living museum, and that its principal purpose "was to break down the social stereotypes that stand between one group and another and help to sustain the power of one over another" (Cantwell 1993:xvi). Others in the Office have characterized the FAF as a "cultural laboratory" or national "family reunion" (ibid.), and newspaper accounts often express a sense of wonder, easy sociability, and celebration:[7]

> Children and their parents roamed the area, clutching canned sodas and ice cream cones, while Junior Cobb, a 30-year-old wood carver from Mount Calm, Ark., patiently hammered on a seven-foot piece of white poplar. . . .

Girls in miniskirts watched elderly women in long summer dresses make wooden dolls. Mobile ice cream stands had the same booming business as the roped-off tents where barbequed buffalo meat was sold.

In one section of the festival, near a platform where the Joe Willie Wilkins blues band of Arkansas was performing, a group of young people talked about how "groovy" the festival was. ("Smithsonian Opens" 1970, cited in Cantwell 1988:v)

A journalist writing about the most extravagant enactment of the annual event, which coincided with the Bicentennial, tried to sum up the tenth FAF with a set of statistics:

Approximately 5,000 participants from 38 foreign countries, 116 Native American tribal groups and 50 unions and labor organizations took part. . . . Nearly 4 million visitors turned out. . . . The total budget came to $7.4 million. . . . About 575 volunteers donated about 60,000 hours of their time to help out the festival's 242 paid staff members.

But all of this would miss the point of the gala summer-long festival. . . .

"We see this as a didactic exercise," says James Morris, head of the Smithsonian's Division of Performing Arts. "It's extremely important to break down the usual assumptions of what culture is, what music sounds like, for example. The variations are enormous, and we wanted to sound the drum for pluralism."

The pluralism was evident throughout the festival, as each week brought a new type of sausage, a new form of bagpipe, a different tasting beer, a new way of dancing, a different way in which to play the fiddle or violin. (Weintraub 1976)

And Robert Cantwell, commenting on a promotional film made for the FAF in 1982, caught some other aspects of what the Festival was about:

This film, it seems, partaking deeply of the post-Vietnam mood, treats the Festival as a kind of cultural summer camp. It finds salutary effects in the Festival for everyone involved; participation in it is, like the great out-doors, somehow good for our health and happiness. Visitors experience the "beauty and joy" of another culture; Native Americans reaffirm their half-forgotten way of life, while other participants find recognition they otherwise would not receive and fulfillment in their reunion with their Old World counterparts. Though the film focusses on the Festival visitor, it tacitly assumes that the Festival, in a general way, revitalizes an almost universal cultural morbidity. (Cantwell 1993:127)

Despite performative differences, one important antecedent of the FAF would seem to be the folk festivals of the 1930s, some of which were explicitly designed to preserve the cultural diversity of American civilization, were already concerned about the levelling effects of commercial records and radio, and regarded folk culture as a kind of endangered species (Cantwell 1988:54). The printed program from the Second National Folk Festival held in Chattanooga in 1935 lists among other attractions: Kiowa dances and singing, Spanish New Mexican song, French folk songs from Vincennes, Indiana, Negro spirituals from Tennessee, Michigan lumberjack music and dances, Ozark mountain music, Negro work songs and games, Tennessee mountain music and games, New London sea chanteys, Arizona cowboy music and ballads, Pennsylvania-German folklore, Kentucky mountain fiddle tunes and ballads, folklore of the Pennsylvania anthracite coal miners, Tennessee square dances, etc., etc.—a mix that would not be out of place at the FAF today. Indeed, the main difference would seem to be the accepted style of presentation: in the 1930s, such festivals consisted of largely non-interactive, concert-like performances on a formal stage (see Cantwell 1988:62–64; the full program is included in Cantwell 1988:56–60), while the FAF, in contrast, actively encourages interplay between performers and visitors.

The FAF's scholar-organizers, many of whom came out of the 1960s folksong revival movement, have written about this broader historical context:

> This concern for the continued survival of folk culture—a kind of parallel to the concern for endangered species in the natural environment—is not a new one. It dates back at least as far as the eminent English scholar, Cecil Sharp (1859–1924). . . . Sharp's insight into the process of cultural preservation was to bring together traditional performers, the wider public and scholars. Encouraging the creative interaction of these three groups within a national institution was the genius of Sharp's work. This interaction has been the motivating principle of the Smithsonian Folklife Program. (Rinzler and Seitel 1977:148–50)

But the FAF—with its mix of entertainment, education, and national politics, presided over by Smithsonian scientists—also harks back to the turn-of-the-century fairs. And it is in those portions of its programs that involve participants from outside the United States that these affinities become sharpest.

Precisely how the FAF got involved in including foreign delega-

tions is not known to us. (American Indians and African Americans—
as well as a diverse set of other "ethnic" Americans—were included
from early on; indeed, the FAF's organizers played an important role in
encouraging greater ethnic diversification within the broader
Smithsonian staff structure.) Some culturally "foreign" peoples were
clearly included as part of the celebration of the ancestral cultures of
various groups of Americans: there have been specific programs about
"Old Ways in the New World" (that included, for example, Greeks,
Tunisians, and Japanese) and the "African Diaspora" (that included, for
example, Trinidadians, Haitians, and Virgin Islanders). But with a staff
that included folklorists and anthropologists whose primary scholarly
research was in Mexico or Tanzania or India, it is not surprising that
programs sprang up to bring performers from such faraway places to
complement the U.S. focus on the Mall.

The introduction of non-U.S. programs exacerbated the representational problems inherent in other Festival presentations. At one
meeting, for example, the director of the FAF expressed concern that
the Smithsonian's Mela—a reconstruction/reenactment of a fair that
accompanies religious festivals in India—would be "an event balanced
uneasily between a presentation, in which there is too much mediation, and a 'cultural zoo,' in which there isn't enough, especially
because the Indians don't speak English" (Cantwell 1993:131). And the
official chronicler of the 1985 FAF described how, in a planning
meeting:

> The issue of the social character of the exhibit site becomes especially
> acute in the case of the eight Kmhmu participants—musicians, spinners,
> weavers, basketmakers, toymakers, and native interpreters. They will be
> placed in a kind of "compound"—a word to which the office's senior
> ethnomusicologist takes strong exception—that will include a garden, a
> blacksmith shop, and a small platform sheltered by a tent. Both the
> director and the state folklorist see potential problems of objectification
> with the arrangement—for the director, the exhibit too closely resembles
> the "cultural zoo" phenomenon of earlier exhibitions; for the state folk-
> lorist the lack of a common language, which would normally provide a
> medium of negotiation between participant and visitor, is paramount—it
> will turn the exhibit in effect into a "living diorama." As a solution, the
> group agrees to redesign the platform so that the visitor, as the director
> puts it, will be "surrounded by Kmhmu," rather than be above them or
> separated from them by a barrier. (Cantwell 1991:153–54)

But this attempt at a technical/presentational solution apparently failed:

> The Kmhmu area, however, became what the state folklorist feared it would, a living diorama; communications between participants and visitors were difficult, and, in fact, except for the old toymaker, the participants tended to ignore visitors as, it seemed, a matter of propriety, actuated by a kind of embarrassment or modesty. To approach the Kmhmu as closely as the Festival setting permits is profoundly disquieting. (Cantwell 1991:156)

On the whole, however, the Festival staff accentuates the positive. Diana Parker, director of the FAF, concludes that "we have learned much in these years . . . since the Smithsonian's annual living cultural exhibition began in 1967 . . . about how to present traditional cultures respectfully and understandably to a broad audience" (1993:15), and Peter Seitel, senior Smithsonian folklorist, also emphasizes "the knowledge the Festival staff has developed about producing living cultural presentations" (1991:495). There seems little question that over the twenty-seven years of its existence, the FAF, and its staff, have continued to change with the times and to learn from their mistakes. The cultural spectacle they produce for more than one million visitors, at a cost of only $1.50 each, is unique. And, however one ultimately reacts to the Festival's living cultural exhibition, there is no doubt that, to borrow Richard Kurin's phrase, it is indeed "a symbol of our own national culture" (1989:20).

*    *    *

We first heard about the "Maroon Program" of the Smithsonian's 1992 Festival of American Folklife from Ken Bilby—friend, former student, and co-participant in the museum-collecting expedition that formed the narrative core of our then in-press book, *Equatoria* (1992). Ken, who had done fieldwork with Maroons in both Jamaica and French Guiana, had conceived an imaginative proposal—to have the Smithsonian bring Maroons from different parts of the Americas together in one place for the first time ever: Saramakas and Ndjukas from Suriname, Alukus from French Guiana, Jamaicans from the Moore Town and Accompong communities, Black Seminoles from Texas and Mexico, Palenqueros from Colombia, and others. It was accepted, and he and Diana N'Diaye, a Smithsonian folklorist, were put in charge of its organization. Much of their initial efforts were focused on raising money to supplement Smithsonian and Quincentennial funds, but they also spent a great deal of time contacting governments and groups who would eventually be invited. Ultimately they made a number of several-week visits—to Palenque in Colombia, to Saramaka and Ndjuka territory in Suriname, to French Guiana, Jamaica, Mexico, and Texas—during which they explained the project, made logistical arrangements, produced videotapes and sound recordings that could be used as part of the program itself, and in general mapped out a series of folkloric activities that would be appropriate for a nine-day period on the Mall. As one part of this pre-Festival planning, they visited us in Princeton, where we were working for the semester, to invite our participation as what the FAF calls "presenters" for the Saramaka participants (or "tradition-bearers," as the FAF dubs them) and ask us to write brief essays for the program book that would be on sale to visitors.

The idea, according to FAF internal planning documents, was that

> Visitors to the Festival will be able to learn from present-day Maroons about their techniques of hunting, fishing, and cultivation, as well as basketry, foodways, and herbal medicine (for which Maroons everywhere are famous). The Festival program will also feature performances of music and dance and other demonstrations illustrating that the notions of cultural continuity and cultural innovation are not necessarily in conflict, and indeed, may at times be complementary. (Presenter's Notebook for Maroon Program)[8]

The FAF's broader goals in hosting Maroons included

> honoring and commemorating the African presence in the New World. It is also intended [to] . . . open a dialogue between the different Maroon communities; providing a forum in which Maroons from different countries can discuss ways of meeting the challenges affecting their societies. (ibid.)

The same document outlined the planned physical arrangements on the Mall:

> The site is built loosely around the concept of a village with various "family compounds" representing the Maroon communities sending representatives to the Festival. Guiana Maroons, Aluku (Boni), Ndjuka, and Saramaka, will be located in the same general area because of their linguistic and cultural proximity, however three structures—two house fronts and one entire building—will be built to reflect the unique architectural features of dwellings of each group. The three will share a kitchen space. (ibid.)

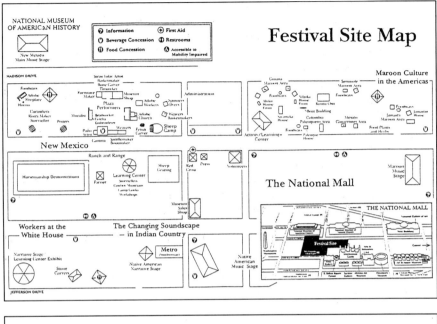

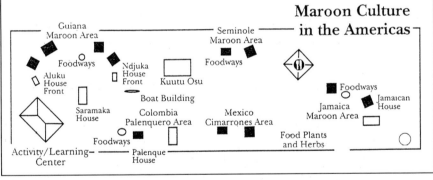

Fig. 2 FAF maps from the Presenter's Notebook

Meanwhile, the role of presenters was spelled out in some detail in a specially prepared booklet that provided background on the FAF as well:

The Festival has two immediate goals:

1) To honor the participants and the cultural groups they represent through display of their traditional arts, skills and knowledge—and thereby encourage their efforts.

2) To make a broader public aware of the rich variety of cultural traditions, the value of cultural diversity and continuity, and the obstacles impinging on traditional cultural practice.

The Festival has pursued these goals since 1967, and our knowledge of how to present cultural traditions has increased over the years. . . .

*The Festival is designed to foreground community tradition-bearers themselves*: musicians, storytellers, craftspeople, cooks, ritual specialists, skilled workers and others. . . .

*Your role as presenter is to enhance the participants' presentations at the Festival and facilitate their communication with the broadly defined audience that attends this event.* . . .

At the Festival you as presenter verbally (and sometimes visually) construct the interpretive *frames* in which participants can be well understood by a general public. . . . *Thus it is a presenter's responsibility to link a particular participant's or a group's knowledge and history to the overall contexts of their culture, home community, and customary setting for the activity presented.* (1992 Presenter's Guide:2–5, original italics)

The Presenter's Guide contained much other useful information, including what, for purposes of the FAF, is and is not to be considered "folklore." Presenters were told, for example, that even when performed by "tradition-bearers,"

*Inappropriate items for presentation are those taken directly from the repertoires of pop culture or elite culture.* . . . *Also inappropriate for Festival presentation are items from traditional repertoires now performed in an acculturated style oriented toward non-community, tourist or out-group audiences.* (1992 Presenter's Guide:8, original italics)

Despite our intellectual inclination to problematize various aspects of what we were learning about the FAF, we felt personally supportive of Ken's initiatives. We also looked forward to seeing some Saramakas, even in the anomalous context of a Washington summer. Besides those Saramakas we had known for many years, there would be Maroons from other groups we had met before: some of the Alukus who figured in our *Equatoria* expedition and Colonel Harris of the Moore Town Maroons of Jamaica, whom we had visited years ago. We were especially looking forward to meeting the newly installed Paramount Chief of the Saramakas, Songo Aboikoni, who had been represented by a triangle on our genealogies since the 1960s but was away on the coast whenever we had been in "the field."

In the days after Ken and Diana's visit, we kept thinking about the history of "exhibiting people"—stereotyped images from *Aida* and *Alexander Nevsky* of dejected war prisoners being paraded through the streets as trophies, the great nineteenth-century colonial exhibits, the American circus shows. Though scientific racism has long been dead, and the current ideology of the FAF is now what Bauman and Sawin call "liberal pluralism,"[9] the imprimatur of its anthropologists for "living exhibitions" certainly created a strong link, in our minds any-

> America is not an aggregate of little semi-hostile communities antagonistic in feeling and welfare. . . . We belong to a united and homogeneous Nation, one in aspiration, one in feeling and one in interest. . . . There are no bad Americans. . . . We are all good; and the better we are acquainted the more we like each other. (The Portland *Oregonian*, on the occasion of the Lewis and Clark Centennial Exposition in 1905, cited in Rydell 1984:206)

> In affairs like this we realize our strength. We realize how beautiful we are. Black is beautiful. Appalachia is beautiful and even old, tired, Washington sometimes is beautiful when the American people gather to sing and fall in love with each other again. (Alan Lomax at the FAF, 7 July 1968, cited in Kurin 1991:9)

way, with these complex pasts. And we weren't yet sure that some aspects of hidden ideology might not have persisted, from the turn of one century to the next, as well.

We also reflected on our only previous brush with touring Maroon performers. In 1981 we were asked by the Museum of Cultural History at UCLA whether, in conjunction with the exhibition of Maroon arts we were curating there, we would like to bring up a group of performers from Suriname. We declined that offer on the idea that it would be difficult for us to assure a proper reception for them so far from our own home, but decided to plan such a visit for the next year, when the art exhibit would be in Baltimore, where we then lived. With NEH support, we arranged for a group of nine Saramakas to spend about ten days with us, presenting a total of four hour-long performances (two in Baltimore, one in Washington, and one in New York). The whole group lived in our house throughout, sleeping on mattresses on the floor; we cooked communally and traveled together in a rented van. A troupe of African American dancers who attended the first performance became friends and spent several evenings socializing at our house with them.

Those 1981 performances were semi-didactic; they were introduced by a ten-minute slideshow about Saramaka culture, and each

song or dance was contextualized either by one of us, or by the
Suriname ethnomusicologist who accompanied the group. All in all,
the work load was limited, the visitors ate familiar foods they chose
and cooked themselves, they were paid for each performance (following NEH norms), and there was plenty of time for socializing informally with Americans, shopping, and sightseeing together in Baltimore and New York. Our familiarity with their culture and language,
the relatively small scale of the operation, and our control over what
happened each day meant that we could pretty well assure the group a
positive experience.

Nevertheless, the spectre of a cultural zoo still hung over the
enterprise. While from one point of view we, as anthropologists who
had lived for a couple of years in the villages of these same people, were
finally getting the chance to return their hospitality, we were, from
another perspective, playing the role of cultural impresarios. Even in
what we thought of as the "best case scenario," the risk of objectification haunted the enterprise. How would that risk play itself out in a
large public festival on the Washington Mall?

Before long, we had a very useful, several-hour-long meeting with
eminent folklorist Roger Abrahams, who was visiting Princeton for a
symposium. We told him about our invitation to participate in the FAF
(which he had been involved in since its inception), and laid out some
of our uncertainties. He spoke of his commitment to folklore as a
discipline, to the practice of public folklore, and to the Office of
Folklife Programs—which he explained was in the throes of an administrative transformation within the Smithsonian and was about to
become the Center for Folklife Programs and Cultural Studies. Then he
strongly urged us to participate in the FAF—in order to write about it
reflectively and thus contribute to its betterment. Roger argued that
the Festival staff itself often lacked the kind of perspective that outsiders could bring to the event, and he alluded in passing to a collective
defensiveness sometimes exhibited by the organization.[10] He had read
*Equatoria* in manuscript and knew of our interest in forms of represen-

> For their part, folklorists working in the public sector are often so
> overextended and so dependent on fickle government funding that
> they lose sight of the larger enterprise—the emancipatory poten-
> tial of folklore as praxis, that is, how what we do as folklorists can
> be of socially redeeming value in ways that go beyond celebration.

> Indeed, dependence on government funding shapes the language
> of advocacy and blunts its critical potential. (Kirshenblatt-Gimblett
> 1992:33)

tation. "Where else in the modern world," he teased us, "can you still see systematic exhibitions of people?"

We decided to go ahead. In accepting Ken and Diana's invitation, we let them know about our conversation with Roger and told them we hoped to include a chapter on our Festival experience as part of a book on museums and cultural representation that we were planning to write.

Roger had mentioned a manuscript about the FAF he found insightful, by a man named Robert Cantwell, that was under consideration at the University of North Carolina Press, and he eventually arranged for Rich to be one of the readers for the Press. So, via Cantwell's bibliography and analysis, we were soon introduced to prior reflections on the Festival—its history, its ideology, the whole remarkable story.

One of the things that struck us, in the various documents that emanated from the Festival and its originators, was the contradiction between its vaunted populism and implicit elitism, that quintessentially American territory that Larry Levine has explored so well in *Highbrow/Lowbrow* (1988). The "us" versus "them" (civilized versus primitive) dichotomy that hounded anthropology's first hundred years as a disci-

> The statement the Festival makes is an important alternative to
> elitist cultural models which would have us believe that one is not
> "cultured" unless one attends the opera, reads Proust, knows the
> contents of the museum of "art." (Ralph Rinzler, Festival Director,
> 1976, cited in Cantwell 1988:113)

> Folk revivalism is deeply bound up with social class and with the
> prestige accorded to those cultural forms endorsed or valorized by
> culturally influential people and institutions. It may seem immedi-
> ately paradoxical to say that folklife, normally identified with lowly,
> marginal, and disadvantaged peoples, should occupy a position of
> social prestige. . . .
>     The folk revival in every phase consisted of the representation
> of folklife by influential people and institutions: by photographers,
> writers, and collectors; by social reformers and educators; by rich
> aficionados such as the Rockefellers; by museum curators; by
> Franklin Roosevelt, his government, and its culture workers; by
> the commercial record, radio, and broadcast establishment; and,
> in our own period, by the Festival of American Folklife. . . .

> In this context, "folklife" is an elegant, exquisite, or mandarin
> cultural construction whose venue is the esoteric or connoisseur's
> record label, the gallery-quality photograph, the avant-garde
> publication and broadside, the bohemian coffee shop with graffiti
> from Nietzsche and Wittgenstein on its walls, the university
> concert hall or common room, the summer watering spot like
> Newport with its weekend folk festivals, and, of course, the
> Smithsonian and the Library of Congress; at a deeper layer in its
> history lies the country dance society, the outing club, the private
> preparatory school, and the left-wing summer camp. (Cantwell
> 1993:234–35)

pline seemed equally strong in the field of folklore. And many of the
subtle problems of "gaze" that Sally had analyzed in the world of
"primitive art" (1989) reappeared in this different guise. Issues of taste,
power, and who were the definers and who the defined abounded.
Many of these issues seemed under-acknowledged in the folklore
literature; class, power, and conflict were often occluded in favor of
varied conceptualizations of celebration, festivity, and communitas.

By the time the semester ended and we had returned home to
Martinique, we had learned a good deal about the exhibiting of people,
including that done since 1967 by the Smithsonian in our nation's
capital. We began to keep a diary, in anticipation of writing about our
upcoming experience.[11]

\* \* \*

*8 June 1992, Anse Chaudière*

Just off the phone with Diana N'Diaye, who called to work out
some of the logistics for the upcoming Festival. She said one of the
most important things for us to do was to sit down with the Saramakas,
soon after their arrival in D.C. and, as she put it, "discuss with them
how they would like to represent their own culture" in terms of such

> In planning this research [on the FAF] . . . we also recognized that
> the requirement to re-present or re-create for an audience behav-
> iors that have their primary existence in other social settings could
> be a significant factor in participants' responses to the festival.
> Our research revealed, however, that the necessity of making the
> kinds of practical and intellectual readjustments required by the
> festival frame assumed even more prominence than we had
> expected. (Bauman et al. 1992:14)

things as cooking, singing and dancing, and leadership. She also had a number of specific questions. What are some Saramaka plantain recipes? What spices do they use? What kind of sewing thread should she have the Smithsonian obtain for demonstration use? How many peanuts should they buy? "As presenters," she told us, "your job will be to bridge between the audience and the participants, to frame the presentations." Also to conduct public interviews with the participants. We

> Among the most challenging tasks of the Festival presenter is that of presenting the traditions of participants who speak languages other than English. . . . You can alter the audience experience from an observation of the "exotic" to a real opportunity for understanding and person-to-person communication. Begin each session by teaching the audience a simple word or two of greeting with which to welcome the participants. (1992 Presenter's Guide:18–19)

are charged with "building the conceptual bridges to understand what the traditions are about"—in performance, foodways and crafts, and interviews on the "narrative stage."

In response to her queries, we came up with the following sorts of advice: Ask the Maroons to bring cooking utensils (wooden food stirrers, branch swizzle sticks for okra, etc.) if you're going to ask them to show how they cook; ask them to bring serving dishes (banana leaves, calabash containers, etc.) if you're planning to stage an ancestral feast; ask them to bring *maipá*-palm oil if you want the food to have a Saramaka taste; get some fine sand that they can pretend is cassava flour for the demonstrations of cassava cake designing; ask them to bring peanut grinding boards and gourd rollers so they can show how they grind peanuts for their festive dishes. Be sure to have Maggi and Aji-no-moto, limes, and okra on hand; use pork and beef in place of game meats. After we explained that Saramakas cooked cassava on large round griddles and Ndjukas on small oval ones, Diana expressed concern about whether Saramakas would be upset if they were asked to cook cassava cakes on Ndjuka griddles.[12] She also said she'd arranged to get calabashes from Hawaii because they couldn't (or weren't allowed to?) import them from Suriname.

After our phone conversation, Diana faxed us the day-by-day schedule of the Maroon program, arranged under the headings of "music and dance area," "narrative area," "activity center workshops," "ongoing demonstrations," and "foodways"—prefabricated categories designed to fit Maroon realities into user-friendly, marketable packages for Washington D.C. Thus far (since she had to free her phone line after a half hour this afternoon) she has not told us what is supposed to happen, for example, during the "Narrative Area: Kuutu Osu [Council House]" presentation of "Tales of Maroon Ancestors" or "Women in Maroon Cultures." But she has promised to call again tomorrow.

Vivien Chen, who's in charge of the Activities Center, has also been calling us for advice. Our discussions have resulted in decisions to use pre-cut construction paper for children's classes in patchwork design (thus avoiding sharp needles) and modeling clay for the "wood-carving" activities (ditto for knives).

*Tuesday, 9 June 1992*

Another long phone call from Diana. She explains that for each part of the site there is a Foodways Coordinator, and asks us for recipes that she can pass along. We discuss the variety of Saramaka snacks and festive dishes, and suggest that she have available plantains, sweet potatoes, peanuts, etc. She also mentions that she has decided to ask Saramakas to bring their own calabashes after all.

Then her description of "The Site": "We have one generic structure for Saramakas, another for Ndjukas, and another for Alukus," she tells us, and asks whether we have any suggestions for what to put in these structures, where people will be doing things like demonstrating hair designs or carving. She explains that what the FAF calls a "generic structure" is a three-sided box with a roof and sides in latticework. "We've used them for a couple of years. People basically come and transform them and decorate them. . . . In some cases, people use

However admired they may be, moreover, however well remunerated, the artists are in a position of apparent internment, even servility, and visitors often speak of them, and observe them, as if separated from them by a one-way mirror. . . . The visitor, too, is isolated from his or her individual history and community and can perhaps feel frustrated to have been placed in circumstances that imperfectly represent, or seem to misrepresent, him or her *to the participant*. (Cantwell 1993:155, original italics.)

chairs. They can leave stuff inside when they're busy somewhere else. We know that they're coming to an exotic place," she continues, "with people around all the time. Having a place to call your own can be very important, and the generic structures provide that. They sort of evoke a set of houses, a village. I say 'sort of' because . . . we're not trying to transport a Guiana village here. We're trying to create a context where people can demonstrate the things they do at home, . . . the things they do best. . . . We're not trying to create a *National Geographic* or nineteenth-century exposition village."

The dual threat of the *National Geographic* and nineteenth-century world's fairs' living dioramas has come up several times. We have been told, for example, that "the whole aim of the presenters' contextualization is to keep it from becoming a situation where people are on display. . . . Presenters are there to create context and facilitate communication." And that "the people [tradition-bearers] are there, in effect, as teachers."

We proposed to Diana that there might be problems in our discussing with Saramakas how they would like their culture represented, as she had suggested yesterday. She said she understood that they wouldn't be able to respond in the abstract but that, for example, "They might say, 'This isn't where we would have placed a stool.'" And with time, she assured us, they would get in the swing of things, deciding for example that on a particular day they wanted to cook such and such a dish and not another. "It's been our experience over the years—it's a sort of time-out-of-time event—that people learn quickly what the genre entails and start to make it their own."

Diana also asked us to go over Saramaka dietary restrictions, food preferences, and eating habits in as much detail as possible so plans could be made with the hotel. After talking about Saramaka diet more generally, and pointing her toward things we'd written on that subject, we said that there were really only two important requirements: that there be a lot of white rice (but really a *lot*, Sally stressed) at every meal—Saramakas use the same word for "rice" and "food"—and that there be soup spoons, since Saramakas are not used to eating with knives and forks. Pressed further about what would be culturally appropriate in the way of spices, meats, vegetables, fruit, and drinks, we argued that such refinements weren't important: "Just be sure to have rice and large spoons at each meal, and they'll be fine."

*Tuesday, 23 June*

Flew to New York yesterday and picked up our old yellow Toyota, left at Rich's mother's for local transport. This morning we drove to Baltimore, where we met Adiante.[13] Like us, Adi has been invited by the Smithsonian to serve as a presenter in the Maroon program. He loaded a few carvings as samples of his work, plus a stack of business cards, into the car, in the hope of drumming up some commissions. Then on to Washington and across the Potomac to the Keybridge Marriott.

As we were checking in, the Suriname delegation arrived, straight off a plane from Miami. Mass confusion in the lobby, with American Indians coming and going. Men in cowboy hats and boots, string ties, and silver belt buckles. Jamaicans, Dutch-speaking urban Surinamers, Smithsonian volunteers (many with visible cultural roots in the 1960s), hotel workers, and miscellaneous tourists, all surrounded by suitcases, drums, burlap sacks, and other festival-producing paraphernalia.

For us it's an exciting reunion with friends we haven't seen in years. Aduengi, Assistant Headman of Dangogo (the Saramaka village we called home for two years in the 1960s) and one of the star performers in our book of Saramaka folktales, had lost some teeth and gained some gray; he'd been assigned responsibility for accompanying Chief Songo, to assure his comfort and security. Ayumbakaa, a teenager when we lived in Dangogo, had been part of the first generation of boys to attend (at least occasionally) the mission school a half-hour downriver; now, he had recently been made village headman, and was also gray-headed. Anike Awagi, Saramaka elder and ritual specialist, had served as leader of the performance group that stayed in our house in 1981, as well as most other touring Saramaka cultural groups; still brimming with energy, he has long been an active woodcarver, drummer, and cultural promoter.

We didn't recognize Akumayai, from a village near Dangogo, but she had distinct memories of seeing us on the river when she was twelve or thirteen. Aliseti, the oldest of the four women, introduced herself as a wife of Kantjan, the virtuoso dancer who was part of the

1981 performance group, and said she had heard many a story of his stay in Baltimore. The other women were Patricia and Kayanasii, and the star dancer was Djangili, an athletic performer who boasted he had been a professional boxer for a time in Cayenne. We were formally presented to Chief Songo, who reminded us of the late Chief Agbago, his mother's mother's brother, in both physical appearance and demeanor. We also introduced ourselves to the seven-person Ndjuka contingent, including Paramount Chief Gazon, whom we had once met in Paramaribo in the 1960s.

A piece of luggage belonging to Aduengi is missing, and frantic efforts are made to trace it. The whole assemblage is centered around the front desk, where clerks are attempting to assign room numbers and distribute keys: many of the people they're checking in answer to names different from those on the official list provided by the Smithsonian, don't understand English, are not literate, and display not-so-subtle signs of excitement and culture shock.

The Maroons are put two to a room, spread around the hotel, with some last-minute negotiating about who will room with whom. They're quick to orient themselves in terms of hallways, elevators, dining facilities, and each others' whereabouts within the general labyrinth, and to master the technique for swiping the plastic cards in their locks to produce a green light and thus gain access to their rooms. Chief Songo gets a quick lesson from Rich in how to work the hotel plumbing; though he is familiar with toilets and showers, the details of these American models are new to him. Meanwhile, Sally goes over switches, knobs, and handles with the women, who are particularly taken with the color TV.

Just before dinner, Patricia discovers that her wallet is missing. In her room with the other women, she's turning her luggage inside out, pawing through clothes and toiletries, nearly hysterical. When Sally goes by the room on the way to dinner, Patricia says she can't possibly eat; her whole life has been ruined. The contents of the wallet included large sums of money, in dollars, from various friends and relatives who had asked her to buy particular items, from face creams to radios, in the U.S. Rushing down to the dining room, Sally reports Patricia's distress to the others. Djangili smiles and says he took the wallet when Patricia left her hand-luggage unattended in the airport; it has been safely tucked away in his pocket the whole trip. After this, he says, she'll do a better job of remembering his instructions to the women to keep their valuables with them when they travel.

The hotel's grand ballroom is set up with large round tables to feed the several hundred Festival participants, buffet-style. An FAF official checks people off a list at the door. After loading their plates with an array of unfamiliar foods, the group colonizes a couple of tables and attempts to master the art of eating with a fork. Amidst the colorful crowd, we pick out a table of Alukus, and go over to greet them. We know four of the nine performers from a visit to Aluku in 1990; in addition there's Abienso, the mayor of Maripasoula who we met during that trip, and Gaanman Adochini, to whom we are formally introduced for the first time. The Saramakas get a real kick out of being served by uniformed hotel staff, who make the rounds with pitchers of water, tea, and coffee. And there are animated reports by Ayumbakaa and Djangili—the first to return to the buffet for dessert—about the available choices. Jello proves particularly difficult to gloss in Saramaccan.

# On the Mall

*Wednesday, 24 June*

It's "training" day, with a visit planned to The Site. But first, a general breakfast meeting in the grand ballroom for everyone involved in the Festival. All presentations at the microphone are in English, with running translation into Spanish for the large New Mexican delegation.

James Early, Assistant Secretary of the Smithsonian, makes a speech about "traditional family values," saying that "we all know how important these are today for raising our children. We need to show them the strength you [the tradition-bearers] still have, as a lesson to all of us." He welcomes "the family of cultures from around the world," and asserts that "the Festival is especially important when the world is groping for values." Then Richard Kurin, Director of the Center for Folklife: "Behind these objects in the Smithsonian museums are people. Our most valuable treasures are not made of stone, not made of fabric,

> The tall, distinguished-looking Ralph Rinzler again approaches the podium [addressing the "tradition-bearers," at the beginning of the Festival]. . . . "You are going to become a community in yourselves, and relate to the community outside. . . . We hope that what will happen is that you will communicate across all sorts of barriers and reveal the real genius that is in each of you." Peter Seitel [Director of the Office of Folklife Programs] amplifies Rinzler's point: "The Smithsonian is the National Museum of the United States. Its purpose is to present things of importance in science, art, and the humanities. . . . We feel that the traditions you people carry on are as important as a lunar lander or the work of sculptors and painters." . . . Margie Hunt, who heads the Cultural Conservation program . . . concludes by saying that she feels honored to be in the presence of so many brave, gifted, and accomplished people, and she hopes that the Festival will honor them in return—a remark that inspires a spontaneous burst of applause. (Cantwell 1993 [describing the 1985 FAF]:142–44)

but of flesh. You'll have the opportunity to tell your story, to share your wisdom, to one and a half million people. There is no script; you can tell it through your own crafts, your own music, . . . [In the history of the Festival,] 16,000 people from around the world have come to the Mall to tell their stories." There's a great deal of talk about wisdom: "It's too valuable a gift to lose. And if we can help, we hope to do that."

Diana Parker, the energetic director of the Festival, offered greetings in the nineteen relevant languages, hastily written on a card by someone who had gone from table to table soliciting them. *Welcome! Wada-oo! Bienvenue; Lolma e'quatsim; U kó mbéi piízii [sic] ku únu; Hinzhiw; Gu'a'dzinah; Tonshee; Bienvenido; Hee ya who* . . . and so on.[14] At our table, at least, the tradition-bearers did not recognize the syllables intended for them. "We started with grass and trees," she went on, "and built a little village that we hope will make you happy. We are here to make this work for you. You've come to visit us."

> In the art museum or out on the National Mall, it is social privilege or the sense of it, projected by the accumulation of cultural capital, which a museum or a folk festival represents, that permits the naked exposure of the object as object, or the folk as folk, plucked out of the cultures and communities in which they are at home. That folk artists themselves might feel honored or legitimized in the transaction is not at issue; such effects are on record and form an important element of the Festival ideology. In the Festival of American Folklife the limits of museum display have been expanded, but in order to expand them it has been necessary to expand, too, perhaps, our willingness to objectify people socially "below" us, and to coax out their complicity in the process. (Cantwell 1993:154–55)

After the breakfast meeting, the several hundred Festival participants mill around the Marriott lobby waiting for the buses to arrive. The Saramakas are asking us when they will have time to go shopping, to walk around Washington, to see America; Diana N'Diaye asks us to tell them that she understands how anxious they are to have their first view of the Festival site. We tell the chiefs, who have been sitting together in the lobby, that they can board first, and then make sure that no Saramakas, Ndjukas, or Alukus are left behind. There's an air of anticipation and excitement as we cross the Potomac. The men are speculating about the river's fishing, and the women launch into a *sêkêti* song they had made up the day before about the Miami airport.

The Mall is sleepy on this summer morning, as the whole Maroon contingent strolls across to the area that will be theirs for the next ten days. The generic structures look bare and forlorn and damp. The Maroons, including the Jamaicans, Colombians and Seminoles, are told to gather in the *"Kuutu Osu"* (a.k.a. Council House) for instructions; Diana speaks in English, Ken in Aluku. Diana stresses that the goal of the event is "to honor Maroons from all over the hemisphere." Though the Festival hasn't yet begun, it's a message that we have already heard quite a few times. One of the opening speeches includes a remark, apparently planned ahead of time with a sweltering Washington summer in mind, apologizing for the uncomfortable weather: "I know it's terribly hot here today. . . ." But in fact there's a distinct morning chill in the air, and many of the tradition-bearers who've come from tropical climates are looking for jackets or some other form of warmth. Diana tells the Maroons that they have been "enormously creative," and that their ancestors fought for freedom. Also that the different groups have much in common with one another. "We know there are foods that you prepare the same way, and drum languages that you share."

The special presenters' orientation meeting is also held in the "Narrative Area - *Kuutu Osu.*" We receive instructions to advertise T-shirts, crafts, and books, and to acknowledge the Program's sponsors at every microphoned opportunity. Rich feels reluctant to take on the role of T-shirt salesman for the Smithsonian, but helping Maroons sell their woodcarvings, calabashes, and textiles is a job for which we feel genuine enthusiasm.

It's preliminary payday at the administration trailer on The Site, the time for all participants and presenters to get photographed for their dog-tag IDs and paid a small advance (ours as presenters is $110 out of a total for the Festival of $810). Maroons, like other participants, stand in a long line in the sun waiting their turn. The chiefs have to wait along with everyone else. Once inside the trailer, it's airconditioned

> It's beastly hot, and the participants, some of them elderly men and women, have to stand in a long line in the sun and dust outside the administration trailer to get the advances they need to get settled in Washington. They should get them in personalized envelopes, I complain to Charlie Camp, waiting for them in their rooms. They are guests, I insist—guests, not employees.
> "Wait until you see the reception at the Castle," he says. "They're invited for the amusement of the VIPs and some of them don't even have time to wash up. After spending all day out on the Mall." One

> year, he remembers, a group of participants, tired of being treated
> like animals on the Festival site, refused to ride in the bus pro-
> vided to transport them to the dormitories: a vehicle from the
> National Zoo that, until they covered the words with a magnetic
> sign, spelled out "ZOO BUS" in giant letters across its sides.
> "Welcome to the Plantation," Charlie says. (Cantwell 1993:144–45)

and the Saramakas say they're freezing. Complications in matching up
people's names with the computer printouts the Smithsonian has
compiled. Maroons from Suriname laboriously sign their names or
place x's in exchange for cash. We translate and give instructions and
try our best to lubricate this joining of nonliteracy and high-tech.
Henceforth, the ID tags, worn as necklaces, will grant the right to eat
lunch on The Site.

A good part of the day is spent unpacking and setting things up.
Equipment is taken from the crates that had been constructed in
Suriname—drums, costumes, calabashes, large mortars and pestles, a
decorated house front, palmleaf roofing materials, and the crafts items
that individual Maroons have been permitted to bring for sale on
consignment in the Festival's gift shop. A tremendous amount of
preparation in Suriname had already taken place by the time the group
arrived in D.C. Not only had everything from drums and mortars to
rattles and dance costumes been made, assembled, and transported
downriver by canoe, but there had been considerable rehearsal time in
Paramaribo under Awagi's expert leadership. Aliseti told us that each
participant had been given some money (furnished by the Smithsonian)
to buy clothes and shoes appropriate to walk the streets of Washington;
in her case Djangili had helped her implement the purchases.

We spend a couple of hours in the Museum Shop tent on the Mall,
helping Maroons register each table, drum, calabash, and textile they've
brought for sale and decide on an appropriate asking price. Adiante plays
the crucial role here; his knowledge of the U.S. market is unmatched.

The Maroons are instructed to set up their generic structures to
reflect each group's identity. The Saramaka women go to work with
brooms to clean their space and then unpack the colorful plastic and
enamel items the Smithsonian has purchased for the occasion, hanging up cups and other dishware, since they've been asked to evoke an
aesthetically appropriate domestic space. On the back wall they hang

an appliquéd textile and a yellow-and-red banner that says "Surinam Airways" (one of the corporate sponsors for the program). Stools, an *adjíbóto* (mankala) game board, and calabashes are placed around on the table and the floor. Adiante tacks a couple of his own carvings onto front posts, next to a stack of his business cards. And we set out copies of some of the books we've written about Maroons, for consultation by festival-goers.

It's a tired group that boards the bus to return to the Marriott for dinner.

*Thursday, 25 June*

We've been asked to get a shoe size for each Maroon so that flipflops can be provided by the Program; Suriname Maroons, unused to wearing shoes, have been complaining that their feet hurt. At the buffet breakfast on the hotel's top floor, Rich takes a stack of xerox paper and a pencil, methodically goes from table to table tracing every person's left foot, and delivers the sheets to a Smithsonian staffer.

Then off on buses to The Site. Strong sense of being herded. Tremendous amounts of waiting. The Saramaka men are unhappy about the house structure, built by a Smithsonian crew, that they're supposed to complete during the Festival with a thatched roof and decorated façade. It's six meters long, and they had been instructed to cut roofing palms in Suriname for a four-meter structure. Their up-bringing values precision in work-related enterprises, and this kind of sloppiness doesn't sit well with them.

The day's program is handed out to presenters, with each one's particular responsibilities boxed in red; we are supposed to communicate the necessary information to the tradition-bearers under our charge before the gates open to the public. Because it's opening day, things don't get started until noon, which makes the work load less than it will be for the rest of the Festival. The three chiefs from Suriname and French Guiana, who are to be treated as visiting dignitaries, are told that their only job each day will be to sit behind a table in one of the generic houses, except for occasional appearances on the narrative stage to speak on such subjects as self-government and official protocol. Their twenty-three compatriots are assigned, in various several-person groupings, a total of 2¾ hours on the main music/dance stage, 2 hours on the activity stage (aimed at children), 2½ hours on the narrative stage, an all-afternoon "foodways" activity (plantain confections, to complement others in the Maroon area—Texas Seminole corn *suffki*, Colombian Palenquero cornmeal recipes, and Jamaican ginger beer), and ongoing demonstrations of such crafts as stitchery, basketry, woodcarving, hairbraiding, boatbuilding, calfband crocheting, rice and cassava process-

> **Nearly all the natives were accompanied by their women, wives and families, who brought with them all the domestic utensils used when in their native countries, while the men came with their weapons of war and the hunt, their boats, tents, canoes and other paraphernalia . . . so that a complete and most comprehensive idea could easily be had at a glance of just how these people lived when in their own countries. (1894 Barnum & Bailey route book, referring to the "Ethnological Congress" that was integral to that year's circus, cited in Monsanto 1992:23)**

ing, trap making, net weaving, reed plaiting, architecture, interior house dressing, and exterior house decoration.

Lunch will be available from a tent at the other end of The Site, several hundred yards away; participants from throughout the Festival are to walk over at some point when they have nothing to do and queue up for a hot lunch served in styrofoam boxes.

Today's program specifies that Sally is to supervise a 30-minute "house-dressing" demonstration, introduce a 45-minute Ndjuka program on the main stage, conduct an hour-long class on "Guianese music and dance" in the activity center, and moderate a 45-minute discussion of Maroon "healing arts" in the Council House. Rich is to oversee the several-hour plantain project, lead an hour-long session on drum and *abeng* (Jamaican Maroon cow-horn) languages, and coordinate a 45-minute presentation of folktales on the narrative stage.

The program organizers announce, following discussions with the Eastern Maroon participants, that all Aluku and Ndjuka main stage performances are going to be combined, since each of these groups has only two women and not enough active performers to constitute a critical mass. (The artist Lamoraille, for example, came to the Festival mainly to paint the Aluku house facade, and won't participate in performances.) The combination makes sense culturally, since the distance (in everything from language and music to foodways and art) between these two Eastern Maroon groups is much less than between either of them and the Saramakas, who live some distance to the west. But it also doubles their main-stage workload.

The gathering of necessary materials and recruitment of performers for these various activities is up to us; we encounter a variable balance of generosity and procrastination on the part of particular individuals. Aliseti quickly distinguishes herself as a particularly good sport. In spite of being in pain from an abscessed tooth, she performs a spirited *adòmítòtò* dance, mimicking the fluttering of a butterfly from a rump-to-the-ground position. And as an accomplished drummer on stage, she turns out to be a refreshing challenge to gender expectations; we are told by other Saramakas that she also handles a motor canoe in the rapids like a man.

During the morning, thinking ahead to the healing arts workshop, Sally suggests to FAF staffers that comparing Jamaican and Seminole healing will be interesting in itself, and convinces them that Saramaka

> **On narrative stages, make sure that the participants are few in number, so that all have time to answer questions and you have ample time to translate their answers. (1992 Presenter's Guide:19)**

and Ndjuka participation, with its back-and-forth phrase-by-phrase translations, would run the risk of overloading the program. Djangili and Da Molly, who had been scheduled to put in an appearance, are thus freed to devote themselves to the ongoing craft demonstrations. George Huggins loves to talk and quickly engages the audience. The other Jamaican, Charles Aarons, follows suit, though he is somewhat less of a man-of-words. The Black Seminole participant becomes increasingly uncomfortable as the two Jamaican men lead off with a flair, and after a relatively brief set of opening comments she completely clams up. Twenty minutes into the discussion Sally sees tears welling up in her eyes; she is having a serious anxiety attack and when she's

> **Talk stages made many of the participants feel uncomfortable and objectified. (Bauman et al. 1992:42)**

asked gently if she'd like to respond to one of the questions posed from the audience, she shakes her head and presses her lips together in an effort not to cry.[15]

The session on "Anansi stories" in the Council House, moderated by Rich, also ran into problems. The Ndjukas and Alukus had been distinctly unenthusiastic about helping children "try Guianese music and dance" on the activities stage, preferring to do folktales in the Council House and leaving Saramakas to take on the children's demonstration. Rich did his best at interpreting for these Eastern Maroons, but the rapidity of the shouted elliptical nuggets that constitute their tale-telling, combined with the fact that he understands Ndjuka/Aluku only by extrapolation from Saramaccan (something like a Spanish-speaker listening to Portuguese), meant that his running translation missed much of the humor and a good deal of the basic meaning of many episodes. Although he tried not to show it, he felt at sea and frustrated being thrust into this role. Fortunately, John Lenoir, who had conducted anthropological fieldwork among Eastern Maroons, pitched in with his expertise. Afterwards, Peter Seitel, who had been in the audience, remarked to Rich that "presenters have to invent the genre on the spot . . . you have to work out some kind of a voice-over in the narratives, because otherwise it just turns into a zoo," and he physically mimicked people gawking at animals. Rich tried to explain why he hadn't been able to do a "voice-over," but it wasn't clear to him whether Peter understood that these raucous tales were in a language that ethnographers of Saramaka aren't prepared to handle except in a much more user-friendly form, such as direct conversation.[16]

One of the striking things about the four Saramaka women is that between performances they're able to sit together in their assigned space, embroidering, making calfbands, and chatting, while groups of twenty or thirty people come and go and stare at them. Talking to each other as if they were in one of their own villages, as if no one else were there, they manage to block out the festival scene for long periods.

> **The public purpose of zoos is to offer visitors the opportunity of looking at animals. Yet nowhere in a zoo can a stranger encounter the look of an animal. At the most, the animal's gaze flickers and passes on. They look sideways. They look blindly beyond. They scan mechanically. They have been immunised to encounter. (Berger 1991:28)**

Today they seemed really to be enjoying each other's company as they went on and on about the variable amount of time different women have had between their first menstrual seclusion and their first pregnancy, trading personal experiences in animated detail. Festival visitors were looking in at them the entire time, occasionally posing questions about where Suriname was or what language they were talking, which we either answered ourselves or translated to the four of them for replies. But otherwise the women were in a world of their own, far from the Washington Mall.

Occasionally visitors ask about the possibility of going to Suriname as tourists. We have pointed some of them toward Cyril Eersteling, a Surinamer with one Maroon parent who is attending the Festival as a visitor: with offices in the Netherlands and Paramaribo, Cyril organizes "jungle tours" into Saramaka territory that promise exotic adventures in settings of scenic beauty. But other times, depending on mood perhaps, we "break" the rosy "frame" of the Festival as a whole to mention that there has been a civil war going on for the past five years in Suriname, that large numbers of Ndjukas and Saramakas are refugees in French Guiana, and that much of their traditional territory has been despoiled by the national army. Given the nature of the balloon-

> If this year's Folk Festival on the Mall is as good as last year's it will be well worth braving the crowds and the mud. But since Kentucky is the theme of this year's activities, I couldn't help wondering why a display of strip mining is not part of the program—it's such an important aspect of "folk life" in Kentucky.
> May I suggest that such a display would be easy to work up. A couple of big machines could dig up, say, the area of the Mall between 14th and 15th streets. The dirt could be left right on the streets to simulate the destruction of forests, farms, pastures, and yards. About 200 or 300 loads of gravel and rocks could be brought in to make it all more realistic—just dump them anywhere.
> Of course, it would be hard to show the erosion or the mounds of mud which push over barns and houses. But maybe a little stream could be cut through from the river and filled with yellow, stinking acid filth. Or maybe the Reflecting Pool could be substituted. And afterwards, just have them leave it like that for ten years or so. (Buck 1973)

carrying, ice-cream licking festivities at hand, such comments really don't fit. It's as if Serb and Croat and Bosnian Muslim folkdancers were featured in adjoining tents. Things go more smoothly when we block all that out—just as the Maroons themselves do.

Back at the hotel, a late night several-person presenters' meeting is called by Smithsonian staffers in the dark Verandah bar, to plan the next day. Things get pretty tense in a lengthy exchange about a session entitled "New Ways from African Roots: Innovation & Continuities" that Rich is scheduled to conduct on the narrative stage. Should Maroons be asked to discourse on a topic defined in these abstract terms?

> **Formerly, this experience of sharing and participating in traditional celebrations or work practices of an in-group has been the privilege of field workers in the social sciences. The Festival, avoiding an entertainment approach to culture, seeks to serve as a window into community. (Rinzler 1976:7)**

Is it possible to conduct an ethnographic interview and please a crowd of festival-goers at the same time? Some of the program staffers have repeatedly stressed that they simply want the tradition-bearers to act "like they do back home." But to us, asking them to pretend to be back home while speaking into a microphone, on a stage, pausing for translations, in front of an audience, can only produce a charade. Even without getting into the issue of whether "African Roots" is something that Suriname Maroons would choose to talk about in front of a group of unknown North Americans, the request that they reply to questions posed by an ethnographer (about, say, healing practices) for the benefit of an uninformed audience, as if they didn't know that the interviewer possessed a corpus of underlying understandings built up over a long period of time, is asking them to play roles as actors in a parodic facsimile of the ethnographic act. It doesn't come close to constituting an opportunity to "do what they do at home" or permitting them to "choose how they'd like to represent their culture."

The discussion reminds us of another we had recently with a well-meaning French magistrate who tried to get the judicial system in French Guiana to be more attuned to "customary law" differences among the various population groups, by organizing large meetings at which anthropologists publicly "interviewed" native people about their customs. It took the form of posing such questions as: "Among your people, how do you solve disputes?" or "What's your marriage system like?" It assumed people could spontaneously articulate a normative ethnography in terms that would make sense to a French audience. The judge, like the Smithsonian staff, insisted that the process was "empowering" people by letting them speak in their own voices and tell their own stories.

In the Verandah, there are serious differences of opinion on these issues, and fatigue produced by the day's excitement and responsibilities has shortened all our fuses: some of the other presenters clearly think it's inappropriate for Rich to adopt such a critical attitude in this festive

> **A folk festival is idyllic, Barry [Bergey, a folk arts administrator] observes [on the first evening of the Festival]; everyone is euphoric. All the usual fear and mistrust are somehow suspended, and people, no matter how different from one another, find themselves brought together in happy community—so happy, in fact, that even now, at the beginning, it is possible to anticipate the sadness and disappointment when the Festival breaks up. (Cantwell 1993:134)**

context, want to get on with the job, and don't understand why he feels so strongly. The staffers seem ticked off at Rich for expressing his criticisms "in public" and for problematizing things they've worked hard

> **Emma Sickles, one of Putnam's staff members [at the Chicago Columbian Exposition of 1893] raised the only objection to the treatment of Indians that was heard throughout the duration of the exposition, and she was summarily dismissed from her position. (Rydell 1984:63)**

to put together. The group finally breaks up without a real resolution of what will happen tomorrow morning in the Council House.

We fall into bed around midnight, knowing that a cheery Saramaka wake-up call will be delivered at our door in about five hours. It's hard to keep our notes up in the midst of everything else; we're scribbling into pocket-size notebooks and onto the back of our schedules during the day and pounding rough *aides-memoires* into our laptop when we have a few minutes in our hotel room late at night.

*Friday, 26 June*

The second day of the Festival, our third in D.C. Aduengi calls at 5:15 to say good morning; the chief has awoken, he says, and everyone is ready to get started but they need to know what they're supposed to do. We pull on our informal Festival uniforms—staff T-shirts with a Ndjuka winnowing-tray design on the back (which we, like the participants, were encouraged to purchase from the FAF) plus blue jeans and sun hats—and head off with Aduengi, Chief Songo, and the two women rooming on our floor to breakfast, where we meet other members of the Suriname/French Guiana group seated at tables overlooking the Potomac through the plate glass. They would normally eat a meal of rice, root crops, or plantains in the morning, but are making do with ample stacks of what looks like Wonder Bread, slipping northern fruits (mostly apples and plums) into pockets and purses to bring back home to Suriname at the end of the Festival. They've all mastered various essentials such as "good morning" and "thank you," and are having fun trying them out with the servers (mainly recent immigrants who are just learning English themselves) who come around with pitchers of coffee and tea.

Already, the Saramakas are showing themselves to be lively, enthusiastic Festival participants, ready to go and eager to please. The women, especially, win over everyone they meet, with their readiness to sing and dance and to respond to greetings from festival-goers with a warm Saramaka-style embrace.

The flip-flop offer turns out to have represented a misunderstanding somewhere in the staff hierarchy, and Maroons are now being told they will have an opportunity to *buy* them instead on the shopping trip next Wednesday. More generally, a certain number of well-intended ideas fall short of realization: Diana has talked enthusiastically for several days about getting clay so the Saramakas can make hearthstones (since the ones that were supposed to have been shipped were-

> **Although we try to provide the home utensils and ingredients as much as possible, focus on the process and cultural significance of cooking should overshadow concern for exact replication of the home environment. (1992 Presenter's Guide:16)**

n't), and the Saramaka women have been looking forward to the project, but now they're simply making do with cement blocks and no more is being said about it.

There's a pre-opening presenters' meeting in the Council House. Richard Kurin remarks about the Festival, "It's all about foregrounding the people whose traditions are being represented. Make sure to read the presenters' handbook. It may seem a little awkward in places but it represents a lot of collective wisdom."

Today's the first full day, starting at 11:00. Rich's schedule has the controversial seminar on African roots and a session on herbal healing on the narrative stage, a "Try Guianese Music and Dance" demonstration in the Activities Center, and an hour-long program on the main dance stage. Sally is to oversee the cooking demonstration, introduce an hour of Aluku/Ndjuka dancing on the main stage, and lead two discussions on the narrative stage. For the rest of the time we are on duty for the ongoing demonstrations, translating and mediating between visitors and tradition-bearers, and taking care of whatever special needs the Maroons have in the course of the day (obtaining acne cream for an outbreak on Patricia's face, borrowing a chain saw so that the men can shorten some houseplanks, accompanying individual Maroons who haven't yet bought their T-shirts to the administration trailer).

Fig. 3 Try Guianese Music and Dance. Patricia and Kayanasii demonstrating, as Djangili drums. *Photo courtesy Smithsonian Institution Center for Folklife Programs and Cultural Studies*

The Suriname/French Guiana contingent is collectively responsible for 2¾ hours on the main stage and 2 hours in the Activities Center, as well as the day's cooking project ("tying *muungá*"—a labor-intensive processing of sweetened rice, coconuts, and peanuts wrapped in banana leaves and cooked over a wood fire), and participation in six of the narrative stage's nine events: "African Roots," "Tales of Maroon Leaders," "Aluku Maroon Narratives," "Tales of Maroon Heroes," "Ceremonies of Transition (Birth and Death)," and "Herbal Healing." Plus, of course, their ongoing post in the generic structures, where the women sing, crochet calfbands, and embroider, and the men do their best to reply to a steady stream of visitors' questions in English and French, as they work on roofing the "Saramaka house" and installing its handsomely carved made-in-Suriname façade.

For individual tradition-bearers, this meant between two and four hours on stage (dancing/singing/drumming, "narrating," or doing a program for children), a day-long assignment in cooking or housebuild-

> Participants [in the FAF] involved in demonstrating crafts or occupational skills . . . [are] expected to work more or less continuously throughout the festival day and to be prepared to answer questions at any time from the spectators who wander by. . . . Foodways demonstrators, in contrast, rotate through the single demonstration kitchen in each program area, averaging one hour-long presentation per day. . . . Musicians, similarly, usually give one formal, hour-long show per day on the large, elevated main stage which provides covered seating for an audience of 200 or more. . . . Most participants are also asked to appear approximately once every other day on a "talk stage" . . . [for] moderated discussions of the various skills on display and the social and cultural foundations of the various groups in which they are rooted. (Bauman et al. 1992:5)

ing, as well as ongoing crafts demonstrations. Plus the expected informal interactions with visitors.

In the end, Rich made his own peace with the morning session in the Council House by sidestepping the thorny "African continuities" assignment in favor of a straightforward presentation on Saramaka drum language, for which Awagi provided an expert and animated demonstration.

For the 11:45 main stage event, Sally has been told once again to recruit the Eastern Maroons, both Alukus and Ndjukas; Abienso, the Aluku mayor of Maripasoula, is to contribute to planning the program and making the introductions. Abienso, however, is nowhere to be found on the Mall. Heading off to the Alukus' generic structure/home base, Sally disengages them from an in-group squabble and gets them and their instruments to the main stage by the time they're scheduled to perform, with several of the Ndjukas in tow.

At the last minute Thomas Doudou, self-appointed leader now that Abienso isn't there, decides he wants to emcee the event himself,

Fig. 4 Drum language in the Council House. Awagi demonstrating as Rich inter-prets. *Photo courtesy Smithsonian Institution Center for Folklife Programs and Cultural Studies*

in French, with Sally providing a running translation in English. He introduces the performance in flowery Antillian-style discourse. The Alukus, particularly the younger ones, have gotten to a point in the state-sponsored *francisation* process—by attending French schools, lis-tening to Western music, etc.—that they seem aware of many of the implications of "playing Alukus" to U.S. visitors, whether as "dressed up savages" or "freedom fighters." Partly with Ken's help perhaps, they have realized that at *this* festival they are free to play something other than the "age-old traditions" they've performed on their European tours. In some sense, their eyes may be more open than Saramakas' or Ndjukas' to the whole process of "self-orientalizing" involved in cul-tural/folkloric presentations.

The performers are dressed in Western clothes, Thomas explains at the microphone, because they're going to perform a kind of dancing that they now do in couples on Saturday nights. The audience, however, appears to have come for exotic folklore and is less than charmed by the smooth French-language discotheque atmosphere he creates. He repeat-edly invites and eventually pleads with people to come up on stage and join in, but no one takes him up on it. After this contemporary dancing,

Thomas presents more "traditional" Aluku fare. Papa Aneli's *agwado* (stringed gourd) playing, accompanied by singing, was well-received, but Papa Tobu dropped his flute playing after he was unable to produce the sounds he wanted from his recently purchased plastic recorder.

Meanwhile, the Saramaka women were having fun "tying *muungá*" in barely-thawed frozen banana leaves brought over from a Washington supermarket, and gossiping among themselves. They were largely oblivious to the spectators clustered around the roped off cooking area, though while they were shelling the peanuts they began handing out

> It seems clear that the central problem of the exposition as a psychological construction of white Americans was to determine distances and relative placement between peoples, physically and ideologically. Where the gaze can be returned, specular commerce becomes uneasy. Lines must be drawn, and they are drawn in telling ways. On the simplest level, frequently a fence, chain, rope, bench row, or other physical boundary demarcated visitor and performer spaces. Fairgoers spent much time looking over fences. (Hinsley 1991:357–58, describing the 1893 Columbian Exposition in Chicago)

samples, over the ropes, to children in the crowd. Sally alerted them to the Smithsonian's injunction against feeding visitors—the Health De-

> Foodways demonstrations have special presentation advantages and requirements not found in other areas of the Festival. A key advantage is that audience members can usually see and smell the results of the process presented, *even though current Federal health regulations prevent the audience from tasting them.* (1992 Presenter's Guide:15, original italics)

partment's (in-)version of the normal zoo rules about sharing snacks with the monkeys and elephants. The women looked perplexed at the idea of a law against eating peanuts, but didn't insist.

The roped-off cooking area, surrounded by spectators jostling to get a look at what's going on inside, provides one instance of the gap between FAF theory—that presenters can effectively serve as cultural mediators/interpreters between "exotic-looking" people and curious visitors—and reality. The ten (or forty or sixty) spectators are standing around, often at all points of the compass, and we have no microphone. As presenters, we end up either shouting out like circus barkers, "These are Saramaka Maroon women from Suriname"—sometimes we tell their names—"cooking a festive dish called X. It's made with Y, Z, and Q. Would you like to come up and feel the cassava flour?" Or, we talk to a couple of people at a time (leaving the rest in the dark) in a more normal tone of voice, and encourage them, if they wish, to ask questions of the tradition-bearers, which we do our best to translate back and forth. Because of the crowds, and the need to keep answering questions about what's going on here (who the people are, what language they speak, what the ingredients are, how long it cooks, etc.), meaningful dialogue happens much less than it should.

We all gulped our lunches; there was a lot to do and no time to rest. The children's activity, conducted with rattles the Maroons had brought with them, was a great success. And the afternoon dance program, a two-hour sequence for which the Eastern Maroons first donned non-Western attire and performed recognizably "traditional" dances, and Saramakas followed with some excellent *sêkêti* singing and then dances for the snake gods, drew large crowds who responded with enthusiasm.

We're struck by the tastefulness of the costumes the Saramakas have put together for their dances: ordinary wrap-skirts and waistkerchiefs for the women, but all of them matching, and specially-designed halter-like wraps that cover their breasts without looking out of place; the men wear nice-looking breechcloths, shoulder capes, neckerchiefs, and tassled calfbands, just as they would for a dance in their home villages. Meanwhile, the Saramaka women have presented each of us with a home-sewn cape to wear over our T-shirts, a kind of badge of our role as intermediaries.

Late in the afternoon, Sally's charge to serve as co-moderator, with Ian Hancock (a professor of linguistics at Texas who is here as presenter for the Seminole Maroons) for a comparative Guianese/Seminole discussion of "Ceremonies of Transition (Death and Birth)," runs into an unanticipated problem. Ian, who is Romani, explains that it is out of the question for him to moderate, or even be anywhere near, a discussion of childbirth—because of strong Romani notions about gender roles: men must avoid all knowledge of such women's things, and if he were even to participate he would become a laughing stock. Sally therefore moderates the discussion alone. The change turns out to be no problem since the Seminoles need no translator, the women on stage are lively, and the audience is engaged.

Cultural constructions of gender also play into the Saramakas' handling of this session. Before the program is scheduled to begin, Djangili, who has taken on the role of a second leader of the troupe (after Awagi), gives Aliseti a mini-lecture about what he wants her to say. During the thing itself, he sits in the front row of the audience in order to mouth silently the responses she is to provide to the audience's questions about childbirth practices. Thus, although visitors take the session as a demonstration of women's expertise, Saramaka requirements regarding male authority in matters of cultural diplomacy are well respected.

Fig. 5 Sally translates for Aliseti during the comparative discussion of childbirth on the narrative stage. Left to right: Aliseti, Sally, Alice Fay Lozano, Izola Raspberry, Ethel Warrior, Charles Emily Wilson. Djangili is just out of camera range at lower left. *Photo by Shelby Givens*

In general, we're starting to have a better handle on what we're supposed to be doing. And as Diana predicted, the Maroons seem to be

> **Folk festivals display forms of folk culture as conceived by folklorists and other cultural programmers and executed by practitioners they select. (Bauman et al. 1992:1)**

getting into the swing. But the swing of what? Promoting their culture? Acting the parts assigned to them by folklorists? Offering Washingtonians a relaxing and entertaining escape from the pressures of their daily routines? Confirming a happyface image of the Family of Man?

One of the several "insider" visitors is Thomas Polimé, a Ndjuka who has become an anthropologist and lives in Holland. He has been watching the presentation of his culture with interest, and engages Rich in a discussion of how it's going. Rich says he thinks the stage performances are pretty successful—showing their performative stuff is what the Saramakas, at least, really came for. But the business of sitting in little contrived houses and having visitors coming by to stare and

> The spurious, disingenuous quality of artificial settings is, I think, lost on no one and cannot be banished with ever-more-perfect verisimilitude, because the very existence of these settings denies to the visitor the imaginative participation upon which the pleasure he takes in the museum depends; although the introduction of living beings into the structure of a diorama may reverse, in a rather crassly literal way, the awkward morbidity of a plaster manikin, it only amplifies the effect of objectification and domination that is the principal offense of such techniques. (Cantwell 1993:63)

ask questions doesn't seem dignified. Polimé says he was just thinking the same thing: it's the sitting in houses that's a problem.

Later in the day, Djangili spontaneously tells Rich how much the chiefs dislike sitting in their house and being stared at. With an amused smile, he asks, "How do you think President Bush would feel if we brought him to Saramaka, put him in a little house with open sides, sat him down, and invited people from all over Saramaka to come and stare at him?"

> Imagine being installed in a room at an exhibition in, say, Bangladesh, where one's only instruction was to go about one's daily chores just like at home—making coffee, reading the *New York Times*, working at the computer, talking on the phone, walking the dog, sleeping, flossing, opening the mail, eating granola, withdrawing cash from a money machine—while curious visitors looked on. (Kirshenblatt-Gimblett 1991:409)

The Saramakas have made clear to us that for them the central issue at the Festival is dignity. Part of maintaining that dignity is not being a whiner, not complaining publicly to the organizers. If the organizers don't realize when their guests feel they are being treated shabbily, it's not proper for the guests to tell them; that would be undignified. It's up to the organizers to figure it out themselves.

We're more and more aware of slippage between the rhetoric of the Festival and what really happens. As Ian Hancock commented at one point, speaking of the narrative stage, what is called for is "baby talk,"

> I was sitting in an auditorium in Tuxtla Gutierrez, the capital of Chiapas. The auditorium was overflowing with hundreds of people—the ten Chiapanecos who had participated in the Festival [in 1991], their relatives, government officials, scholars and local citizens. It was December, six months after the Festival on the Mall. . . . I was seeing how others had seen the Festival, how members of the participants' communities had construed and represented their participation to folks back home. . . . [The participants] spoke of the importance of the Festival in reaffirming cultural identity and raising consciousness about cultural issues that cross ethnic, national and international boundaries. (Kurin 1992:7)

> The native people from Central and South America [including the Chiapanecos] appeared to have the least open and accessible festival environment—small booths turned away from one another. These craft displays bothered me as almost a zoo with exotic animals on exhibit. (from the otherwise enthusiastic review of the 1991 FAF by Gary Stanton [1992:237]).

not anything related to the presenters' habitual discourse. At the same time, a marked defensiveness shields the Festival staff from dissatisfactions about how the thing is working: "We're only trying to *evoke* what happens back home, not replicate it" is a common line when things fall short. And there's a rhetoric of communal togetherness that, by making everyone responsible, makes no one responsible. We've run into it only once before—in the early '70s when we belonged to a parent-

> Those who champion the folklife festival as a form of representation often number among its virtues that it allows those whose culture is being represented far greater opportunity to talk back to the producers of the representation than is offered, say, by a published ethnography. This may be a potential of folklife festivals, to be sure, but it is rarely achieved in practice. (Bauman et al. 1992:2)

run daycare center whose membership was obsessed with the goal of everyone's participation in all decision-making. Here, we're constantly finding an openness to suggestion, combined with a reluctance to take personal responsibility for specific practical solutions. "Well, if you don't think that's appropriate, you can think of something else." "They" should decide what "they" want to do, "just like back home." And an endless supportive refrain of: "Yes, let's talk about that."

The amount of effort that ends up being ineffectual seems quite high to us, even for an undertaking of this scale and complexity. Staffers have spent hours on the phone with us and with Adi about

> **Misunderstandings and bad feelings arise because participants do not necessarily understand two of the most central staff perceptions of a folklife festival, namely that it is supposed to be a fun and slightly crazy variation from normal work routine and that it operates on an underlying philosophy of liberal respect and cooperation. Staff members are, in a sense, the only ones who really experience what folklorists would call a true festival. Staff and volunteers who come back year after year do so because they thrive on the euphoria of over-extending themselves and on the formation of communitas in a group under stress. They know that festivals always click at the last minute and they enjoy that thrill. Participants are not necessarily prepared for this . . . [and] sometimes don't appreciate what they perceive as unprofessional behavior on the part of the staff, what one participant called "fifteen different people doing fifteen different things and hoping and praying the damn thing works." (Sawin 1988, cited in Cantwell 1988:746–47)**

"appropriate" foods for the Suriname Maroons. Our sole message: people eat white rice, using soup spoons, and nothing else matters. The staffers wanted more detailed information (kinds of spices, specific meats and vegetables), but we insisted that that is all that matters. Neither rice nor spoons were here for our first meal. The dining room workers, including the manager, told us they had never received instructions about either.

We feel as if we're breaking our asses to make everything from stage performances to individual interactions with visitors as successful as they can possibly be, often well above and beyond the official call of duty. Yet we have begun hearing, both directly and indirectly, accusations that we're refusing to transmit visitors' questions to Saramakas and that we're censoring Saramakas' responses. It seems to us that some Smithsonian staffers and volunteers (out of a kind of

> It became evident that some presenters did not feel comfortable
> working in their roles, whether because of individual temperament,
> inexperience with the genres of presentation at the festival, or
> antipathy towards these genres. . . . It is often assumed by the
> festival staff that extensive fieldwork experience, knowledge of the
> conceptual framework of a program, and good intentions toward
> participants will automatically translate into an ability and willing-
> ness to present members of the communities the presenters know
> with sensitivity in the festival context. . . . Clearly this was not
> always the case in the Maroon program. (Bilby and N'Diaye
> 1992a:2)

corporate FAF defensiveness) are confusing our critical stance toward
particular strategies for exhibiting people with the way we are actually
carrying out our duties as presenters.

*Saturday, 27 June*
   A really big day in terms of the size of the crowd, which produces
an especially intensive barrage of oft-repeated questions (where
Suriname is, what a Maroon is, what language they're speaking, whether
it's Spanish, whether it isn't broken French, why the Maroons can't

> Practically everyone who did continuous demonstrations . . . soon
> grew bored with repeating themselves and answering the same
> questions, which grew to appear increasingly inane. (Bauman et
> al. 1992:47)

understand English, what a calabash is, how you play *adjíbóto*). We try
to be friendly and informative, but the Festival setting—with visitors
out to have a good time—makes it a very difficult environment to "teach"

> When I asked an enthusiastic teen-aged Festival-goer for his
> opinion as to the best feature of the Festival, he replied, "The
> Tahitian belly-dancers." Although others might have correctly
> recalled that the dancers were Tunisian, not Tahitian, I wonder
> how many attending the Festival had any idea where Tunisia
> actually is. (Bess Lomax Hawes, "Official Observer's Report,"
> 1974, cited in Cantwell 1988:726)

in. It's uncomfortable to have to speak for (on behalf of) people who
are right there physically but who can't speak the language of the
questioners, especially in this free-for-all atmosphere. The New Mexicans can at least decide for themselves when they want to answer (or

ignore) repeated questions. With so many people asking so many similar questions at the same time, it sometimes becomes awkward for us simply to translate. How many times in the course of an hour can we say to Kayanasii, "Sister-in-law, this woman wants to know if you're speaking broken French" (and translate her answer: "No"), or "Sister-in-law, this man wants to know what you're cooking" (and translate her answer: "peanut rice")?

The Museum Shop still doesn't have the Suriname Maroon art book or the Smithsonian/Folkways cassette of Saramaka music. Sally's assignments are: cassava processing (from grating and extracting the poisonous juice to baking on the griddle); patchwork design in the Activities Center; "Anansi Stories" in the Council House; and Aluku/Ndjuka dancing on the main stage. Rich is to do "Traditions of Self Government" and "Healing Arts" in the Council House. At the morning presenters' meeting, adjustments are made for the fact that at the last moment the Mexican delegation hadn't been able to come to Washington, so their late-afternoon slot on the main stage is transferred to Saramakas, to be introduced by Rich.

The Aluku/Ndjuka group is to follow directly upon the Saramaka performance at 4:45; we're made to understand that holding the main-stage crowd in place is particularly important today, given the size of the expected attendance. By mid-afternoon, however, the Alukus have begun feeling cranky about the whole business. District Commissioner Libretto, listed in the Festival guide as both a presenter and a regional coordinator, had been told to get the group ready, but at 4:40 he's nowhere to be found. To make matters worse, the Alukus and Ndjukas are spread around the Festival grounds, uncostumed and apparently oblivious of the fact that they are scheduled to go on stage. Rich held the Saramaka performance overtime, though the dancers were exhausted, while Sally tried to impress Thomas Doudou with the urgency of the situation; the Eastern Maroons were overdue and needed to hurry, get dressed, bring their drums, and go onstage. Thomas smiled: "What's the matter? Do the Saramakas get tired that fast?" Intergroup tensions (what Maroons call "jealousies") were on the rise. Eventually the Alukus and Ndjukas began to collect their gear, and they were on stage about twenty minutes later. More short fuses as this incident gets relayed to Festival staffers who shared in responsibility for the Alukus;

one of them dismisses it with a condescending smile as exaggerated uptightness on Sally's part.

During the Saramaka dance performance, when things got really heated up, a visitor from the front row jumped onto the stage and joined Djangili for some fast-stepping *sêkêti*. Rich recognized him as Wim Udenhout, Suriname's ambassador to the United States, and announced his presence over the microphone, to polite applause. His name had figured in the documents Rich had been reading as background to a trial about to take place before the Inter-American Court of Human Rights in Costa Rica that pitted Saramakas against the government of Suriname. As Suriname's Prime Minister during the 1980s, Udenhout had taken the stance that when the military murdered civilians (in this case Maroons), it was not in the country's best interests to investigate.[17]

Today the sense of living dioramas was overwhelming. In a crowded Festival space, the raised-platform structures almost become cages. Most visitors don't violate the space, but they do stare in and take pictures, sometimes silently, sometimes making comments and pointing at things they see. At its worst, one might view the Festival experience of the Saramakas as being moved back and forth from cage to stage.

> **Basically, there were two options for exhibiting living ethnographic specimens: the zoological and the theatrical. During the first half of the nineteenth century, the distinction between zoological and theatrical approaches was often unclear. . . . It was not uncommon in the nineteenth century for a living human rarity to be booked into a variety of venues—theatres, exhibition halls, concert rooms, museums, and zoos—in the course of several weeks or months as part of a tour. (Kirshenblatt-Gimblett 1991:402–403)**

A hot Washington day in June attracts enormous crowds to the Mall, and the normal lunch routine would have taken the Maroon tradition-bearers away from their area for a good hour, time which they simply didn't have to spare. So we imposed on a couple of Festival volunteers, from the corps of ever-ready young helpers who lubricate the whole operation, to collect the group's photo-ID tags, drive a golf cart over to the lunch tent, wait in line, and bring back box lunches for the whole gang. When they showed up around one, the chiefs were off at some kind of VIP luncheon, so we and about ten Maroons sat down

Fig. 6 The Saramaka generic structure. Patricia and Kayanasii are peeling cassava tubers. *Photo by Shelby Givens*

to eat in their "generic structure." After handing out the styrofoam boxes, the volunteer carefully arranged the ID chains in a row on the table so each one could be hung back onto its owner's neck before the afternoon's activities resumed. That was when the zoo-sensation began to mount. As we stabbed at our cole slaw with plastic mini-forks, visitors began milling around the edges of the platform, leaning in and making remarks about what they saw. Quite a few took photographs of

> **Members of the audience [at an academic conference] were very concerned about how some of the displays "museumified" craftspeople doing essentially everyday, nonperformance activities. They were distressed at observing live persons put on display as if they were objects. This is the underside of the festival frame. (Karp 1991:285)**

us. Others reached over to the table to finger the ID chains, read out the names, and comment on the facial features in the mug shots. Many inquired who we were, what we were doing, and which exhibit this was.

Our initial reaction was to force a smile, explain that we were eating our lunch, and indicate ongoing exhibits in houses to the right and the left. This tack deterred no one. A few people were irritated to

> The conditions of the meeting of tourists and ex-primitives are such that one predictably finds hatred, sullen silence, freezing out. (MacCannell 1992:31)

learn that we preferred not to have our lunch break recorded on film. Several times people protested indignantly that they were "just looking!" when we suggested they move on to another exhibit. After a while

> **That we objectify culture has long been recognized; festivals, however, also objectify the human performers and implicate them directly in this process. This is an inherently problematic way to confront cultural questions, for spectacle, by its very nature, displaces analysis, and tends to suppress profound issues of conflict and marginalization. The more that ethnographic festivals and museum exhibitions succeed in their visual appeal and spectacular effect, the more they reclassify what they present as art, aestheticize that which is marginal, and risk appealing to prurient interest. (Kirshenblatt-Gimblett 1991:428)**

we decided we had to accept the staring and photo-taking as unavoidable, given the environment that had been created. Like it or not, our box lunches had been defined as public folklore.

> **It is important that you take seriously your identity as an employee of the Smithsonian, a public agency committed to serving a broad and sometimes demanding constituency. This means you should exercise tact and patience in all of your interactions with Festival visitors, as difficult as that will sometimes be. (1992 Presenter's Guide:20)**

Those few times when the roles were reversed highlighted the psychology of being a spectacle. Today the Saramaka women saw a dwarf in the crowd—a young African American woman—and became very excited. To them, she was a "god"—awe-inspiring, something special and unqualifiedly wonderful. One of the American missionaries who has been working in Saramaka since about 1970 is a white woman of the same stature, and she has always been adored and treated with exceptional affection. Now this Festival visitor was stepping into the same role, but without understanding its implications. The Saramaka women dropped what they were doing, ran over, embraced her warmly, and tried to communicate how thrilled they were to see her. She was distinctly uncomfortable at the attention. Clearly, she had come to the Festival to view, not to be viewed. But the

Saramaka women (like the Americans who'd been thrilled to see *them*) were, in their pleasure and excitement, oblivious to her unease.

At another point, the same women looked into the dense crowd of people who were lined up watching them as they sewed, and spotted a pretty child, about four, whose hair was meticulously done up in cornrows. Immediately enraptured, they called out to her in Saramaccan and gestured that they wanted her to come up onto the platform where they were sitting. Each one in turn hugged her warmly and exclaimed at how beautiful she was. Then they decided to give her a present—the nicer of the two calabashes displayed a few feet away. She was sweet and shy. But the incident must have felt awkward to her mother, who took her hand and headed toward another part of the Festival without even a perfunctory thank you for the calabash.

Fig. 7 Hairbraiding in the generic structure. Aliseti and Patricia working on a young visitor. *Photo courtesy Smithsonian Institution Center for Folklife Programs and Cultural Studies*

In the afternoon, the Saramakas did tale-telling with songs in the Council House. One of the high points was a story we hadn't run into before about the Origin of Man's Hair. Awagi recounted how, in the beginning, Woman was alone among humans to possess hair and—patting his head—explained that it was through Her generosity that Man acquired it. Once he got well into the story, Patricia stood up and performed an elaborate dance/mime in which she untangled, combed out, divided into sections, and tenderly braided her (clothed) pubic area. Later, on the main stage, they did some dancing that is performed at home only on special ritual occasions: *mása lámba*, *kêlèwè*, and *adunké*.

At the end of the day, after the stages had been closed down and the crowds had largely dispersed, the Aluku and Ndjuka performers encircled the three chiefs and honored them with a wonderful play of *awasa*; the Saramakas joined in, and ended with some *sêkêti*. The chiefs were very pleased indeed. It was one of those rare moments when the whole Suriname/French Guiana group was participating in a spontaneous celebration of their own, on their own terms and for their own enjoyment. Those spectators who were still hanging around really got a special treat.

The busdriver who took us back has already become the Saramakas' favorite. He asks us to let them know that just for fun he's going to show them a different route. As we approach Memorial Bridge to cross the Potomac, the Saramaka women exclaim at the impressive bronze horse-statues that flank the roadway. By mid-river, they're clapping and singing a *sêkêti* song they've just composed about "the golden horses of the Americans!"

After dinner we took our car from the hotel garage and went for a drive with Djangili, Aliseti, and Patricia. Passed the White House and headed on to Georgetown. Walked the streets, did some window shopping, in and out of a few stores. Went into The Body Shop and looked at their rainforest lotions but Saramakas wrinkled their noses in disgust at the smells in the sample vials and weren't at all interested. "Who are we???" queried a Body Shop/Millennium ad in the window.

*Sunday, 28 June*

Another big day. Adiante spent all last night at the hospital with Aluku Captain Doye's son, Samakon, who was hospitalized after some kind of collapse and had a spinal tap under general anesthesia. At the morning presenters' meeting, Adi's duties for the day are distributed to other presenters so he can catch up a little on sleep.

We're starting to get tired of hearing Festival staffers talk about "breaking frame" while they generally avoid acknowledging that the activities are all "framed" in the first place. There's a lot of talk about giving the participants a chance to "tell their own stories"—as if they could choose their own terms to do so. Also repeated references to having the Maroons "do what they do at home" and "do what they do best." We protest that the whole undertaking of the Festival involves radical selection and framing, but it's not at all clear that this perspective is supposed to be aired while the Festival is in progress.

> **[Once back home in Central Africa] it was hard for the Batwa [pygmies] to convey an idea of the peculiar role they had played at the [1903 St. Louis] Fair. There was no correlate in Africa to the public display of people. Anthropology had not yet been invented there.**
>
> **They turned to Fwela [Samuel Verner, their "presenter"] for help. With his assistance they put on a demonstration of just how it was done. They built the sort of wooden pen they might have used to enclose animals. They put Verner's makeshift rocking chair inside and piled some books on a little table. They added an Edison phonograph and a few recordings. As a finishing touch they added Fwela.**
>
> **He contentedly rocked, smoked, read, wrote, and listened to recordings as he might have on a peaceful day on a porch back home. He was a *muzungu* [whiteman] exhibited in its natural state, its authentic habitat. The Batwa who had not gone to America gawked, stared, and could not help but laugh. What was Fwela doing in there?**
>
> **He was being Batwa came the answer. You who are watching him are being muzungu. Now do you understand what happened there? (Bradford and Blume 1992:139, drawing on Verner's manuscripts now in the archives of the University of South Carolina)**

Looking over the schedule, we see it's going to be an exhausting day; the Guianese Maroons are slated for four programs on the main stage (a total of an hour and forty-five minutes for the Saramakas and the same for the Aluku/Ndjuka group), as well as two of the four activities in the children's area and the usual dose of foodways, ongoing demonstrations, and narrative stage appearances.

Sally's schedule includes an hour of "Patchwork Design from the Guianas" in the Activity Center (for which Aliseti generously converts herself, once again, into an inspired elementary-school art teacher); foodways ("Growing, Processing & Cooking Rice"); and an hour of "Maroon Story Songs" on the main stage. Not sure what was meant by "story songs," Sally discusses the assignment with Diana who says they had had popular *sêkêti* singing in mind. Indeed, this is a rich form of Saramaka gossip, and lots of fun if you can follow the words and know the people being criticized and caricatured. But Sally argues that to an American audience, unequipped both linguistically and in terms of the necessary background information, the songs' apparent repetitiveness could quickly prove tedious and uninteresting. So a decision is taken to use the hour instead to follow up on yesterday's narrative stage session in which the Saramakas' folktales, complete with dancing, singing, and mime, kept a sizeable audience laughing.

Fig. 8 Construction paper patchwork. Aliseti demonstrates as Sally translates.
*Photo courtesy Smithsonian Institution Center for Folklife Programs and Cultural Studies*

Rich starts the day with an hour-long music and dance program by Alukus and Ndjukas; in the afternoon he returns to the main stage for a double feature, with the Saramakas and Eastern Maroons each doing a 45-minute presentation. His Council-House assignment, "Tales of

**On the Mall   57**

Maroon Ancestors," has mercifully been cancelled after his argument that it is absolutely inappropriate to ask Saramakas to talk about as closely-guarded a topic as their history in that public context.

In the morning the Eastern Maroons, with whom we'd had a serious talk about showing up on time, still showed up late. For the second time, Papa Tobu had trouble with his flute and quit after about forty-five seconds.

The ongoing demonstrations start promptly as the gates open at 11:00. Until sometime after noon, there's not a single presenter in the whole Guianas area, since Rich is off at the main stage, Sally is at the Activities Center, and Adi is catching up on much-needed sleep. The demonstrations proceed without interpretation, as in a nineteenth-century exposition village. The Saramaka men have decided to go full steam ahead on the housebuilding, and are using a borrowed chain saw to correct the proportions on the rudimentary structure that had been constructed by Festival workers before their arrival. The women are pounding rice in a mortar, roasting peanuts over a wood fire, and looking forward to supplementing their box lunches with peanut rice this afternoon. Doye was all set to build a boat, but a Festival staffer

> The Royal Asiatic Society of Bengal . . . proposed to the government that an ethnological congress be held . . . and that "as they [the Aborigines] are such excellent labourers, they might be utilised as Coolies to put in order the Exhibition grounds at certain times, while at others they take their seats for the instruction of the Public." (Prakash 1992:157–58)

told him that as a security measure he would first have to cut stakes and build a large fence-enclosure around his work area.

Aduengi has been grumbling about being photographed all the time. Why couldn't the Festival organizers just take a set of pictures and hand them out to visitors who wanted them? People are snapping pictures all the time but Saramakas never get any prints. He would

> [At St. Louis in 1903] the pygmies weren't the only guests of Anthropology who hated being surprised by photographers. Their opposition to the camera was less adamant than that of the Moros, Filipino Moslems who wore "rather repellant expressions" even when they agreed to snapshots. The pygmies, on the other hand, only wanted to get paid. . . . [Anthropologist] McGee signed an order stipulating that anyone who wanted to photograph pygmies had to get a permit from his office. (Bradford and Blume 1992:117)

prefer a ban on picture-taking of Saramakas. The women and a couple of men who are in the generic house agree. Sally pipes up that the Smithsonian has foreseen this as a potential problem and prepared pre-printed signs for participants who desire them, saying "No photographs." They suggest we put one up the next morning.

The hot dusty day, the scruffy lawn, the roped off areas (within which "natives" are plying their crafts—cooking, sewing, chopping wood, hulling rice) look to us very much like their nineteenth-century predecessors. We see little difference except, perhaps, the (theoretical) presence of presenters/translators.

> "I didn't know anyone worked with their hands anymore," said one young girl observing Ben Harris making barrels.
>
> "This is the surest antidote for what ails America down deep," Senator William Fulbright declared. "People here are trying to be creative. Too bad there isn't more of it. Too bad there isn't much consciousness of it. When you live in a city, you forget so easily."
>
> "Look at all those college kids out there," Jimmy Driftwood declared. "They're looking for the roots of our society and where can you find them more than in our folk traditions." (O'Brien 1970)

Fig. 9 A quiet moment at the foodways enclosure. Akumayai and Modillie perform a cooking demonstration. Fire laws apparently require the "sandbox," the fire extinguisher, the chain-barrier, and the presence of a FAF volunteer (Rachel Watkins, standing at far left) to keep visitors outside. *Photo by Shelby Givens*

More logistical disorganization. We were told in the morning that our group should stay at their post and that lunch would be brought by the volunteers in a golfcart; shortly before the Saramakas' 1:30 slot on the main stage, that promise was reversed. So everyone had to run

> **What this boils down to is that there are many different people giving orders and directions about the same matters and that it is often difficult to figure out to whom one should go for information, or whose information is definitive. (Bauman et al. 1992:27)**

across the Mall, stand in a long line, down their lunches standing up (because there weren't enough seats), and manage to be ready, with drums and other props, on time. They made it, barely. They performed

> **On the site, the hospitality area offers a respite from the Festival where participants can rest, talk, eat lunch and get beverages during the day. (1992 Presenter's Guide:22)**

the sinuous, pelvic-centered *gogó baléta*, a dance called *kakádeta*, and forest-spirit and snake-god dancing—all strikingly beautiful, we thought. Then some tense moments when the Eastern Maroons scheduled to take the stage didn't show up. A few minutes of ad libbing at the microphone filled the gap while they were being located and brought over.

The "Story Songs" on the main stage played to an absolutely packed house; Sally's interpreting skills met an exhilarating challenge, as the rather bawdy and always unpredictable stories unfolded, got cut off, and gave way to song, dance, and gestural comedy. For both performers and audience, it was a fast-paced hour.

After the gates closed at 5:30, the Eastern Maroons were scheduled to "host" a one-time-only, end-of-the-day "dance party" on the Native American Music stage. In addition to bleachers, there was a large dance area below the stage for festival-goers to use. Marie-Céline, an Aluku *lycéenne*, whose dancing that morning on the main stage had reflected cooperativeness more than enthusiasm, now perked up with a coy smile and had a lot of fun doing *aleke*, which is what her age-set really enjoys at home. When she's doing "traditional" dancing, which she in fact can do beautifully, she's producing "folklore" and looks like she feels it. But when she can just be herself, her enthusiasm is contagious.

Saramakas, just in from their raucous folktale session, were on a roll, and they joined in at the dance party, too. In the end, the women's inspired performance of *bandámmba*, with spectacularly controlled gyrations of the buttocks, stole the show. At the peak of audience excitement, with the Saramaka women center stage and building up steam, the scene risked getting out of hand, as eager men jumped up to the stage to dance with them, eventually threatening to turn the women's highly controlled sensuality into lecherous body contact. At that point, presenters and staff began to police the stage, forcing the unruly men back down to the dance floor, and the momentum was brought under control. Many men pressed dollar bills into the women's

> **Inevitably, people left their chairs and inched forward to feel the pygmies. All the attempts by Professor Verner and the Anthropology Department to educate the public ended in the same way. The crowds became agitated and ugly; the pushing and grabbing took on a frenzied quality. Each time Ota and the Batwa were "extricated only with difficulty." (Bradford and Blume 1992:119)**

> **It seems to have been quite usual [at turn-of-the-century exhibitions] for visitors to throw money to the performing natives and for the natives to beg for it. (Corbey 1993:344)**

hands or clothes; Akumayai was the hands-down favorite and had netted close to $80 by the end of the evening.

Fig. 10 Crowd at the dance party. *Photo courtesy Smithsonian Institution Center for Folklife Programs and Cultural Studies*

Tomorrow morning is the White House tour. The two staff women checking ID tags for admission to dinner confirm the instructions we have been given several times already: the Maroon chiefs (Aluku Gaanman Adochini, Ndjuka Gaanman Gazon, Saramaka Gaamá Songo, as well as the two Jamaican leaders, Colonel Harris from Moore Town, and Colonel Wright from Accompong) will be picked up by a special van at 8:45 to bring them on a VIP head-of-state tour of President Bush's home. All the other Maroons will board a large bus at nine and be escorted through together. Rich has been asked to interpret for the chiefs.

*Monday, 29 June*

The chiefs are dressed in suits and polished shoes and waiting in the front lobby well before 8:45, but after a while, with no van in sight, Diana comes to announce a slight misunderstanding; the chiefs won't be riding in a special vehicle after all. However, respect for their positions will be shown by having them get on the Maroons' bus before everyone else. Because so much has been made of the privilege of a VIP van over the past few days, the five men are disappointed, but they comply politely with the new arrangement.

Fig. 11 On stage at the dance party. *Photo courtesy Smithsonian Institution Center for Folklife Programs and Cultural Studies*

The bus eventually reaches the White House grounds, but there's confusion about which entrance gate has been cleared for its arrival, and the driver goes from one secret service guardhouse to another, being told each time to try the next one, and eventually circling the entire walled area three times, as the passengers get more and more outspoken in their comments.[18] When we finally get inside the wall and disembark, we find out that the White House doesn't open for another half hour. . . .

The whole group—Maroons from our bus, plus the New Mexican and Indian contingents who have come in other buses—stand on the sidewalk in the hot sun. There's some jostling as people become impatient. Festival organizers come up to Rich to say maybe there won't be a special tour for the chiefs after all, but that they can make it *look* special by having them go in at the head of the line. Eventually that's what happens. The five men enter and shake hands with a young male guide who leads them into a side entrance to begin the tour. As they arrive in the first couple of rooms, each with an announced name (The Blue Room, The Red Room), they are greeted by a black, uni-formed guard/guide. The chiefs assume they are meeting a high gov-ernment dignitary and shake hands with a distinct formality, as Rich introduces them by name, maintaining the appearance of being ac-corded special privilege. In each room, Rich tries to keep up with the guard's patter, translating how Dolly Madison used this room for tea parties, Eleanor Roosevelt used to have meetings in the next, and so on. The chiefs nod politely and thank each guard personally, before moving on.

But by the third or fourth room, the chiefs begin to be overtaken by New Mexicans pushing ahead from behind, and the dignified tour turns into a chaotic free-for-all. Now the chiefs are offended and no longer hiding their feelings. Colonel Harris, whose sight is all but gone and who is getting shoved, seeks out Sally and links arms for the rest of the tour. We begin to hear racial slurs and hostile remarks from the New Mexicans. Why do the niggers always get to go first? Who do they think they are anyway? Fortunately, the *gaanmans* don't understand any of it, except of course the pushing and shoving and the tone of the voices. They ask Rich to please get them through and *out* as quickly as possible. After a perfunctory visit to the state dining room, he does.

> Because the staff works with an ideology of liberal respect for all cultures they tend to expect rather conservative folk to think liberally. (Sawin 1988, cited in Cantwell 1988:747)

> [At the 1876 Philadelphia Centennial Exposition:] Newspapers tried to foster the impression that people from foreign countries were "treated with the utmost respect and courtesy" and that the crowd, above all, was orderly even in the absence of direct military supervision. Generally overlooked were expressions of racial hostility that followed the decorous opening proceedings. (Rydell 1984:14)

They are distinctly miffed but pose for a couple of pictures, taken by other members of the Suriname group, in front of the building. Then, back toward the bus where we again stand waiting in the sun as the rest of the group finishes trooping through the tour.

The *gaanman*s use the time to discuss with each other what they've just been through. They say they are being treated like dogs. Their point of comparison is visits they've made to the Netherlands, where the Queen herself has received them in formal audiences at the palace;

> It is an outrage to put me in a house with common Indians. I don't like my room. I don't get the right kind of food. . . . I ought to have a house by myself. There isn't any room to pray here. . . . Tell the public that when I'm on exhibition over at the [Madison Square] Garden I don't like to be laughed at. . . . What do you people think a Hindu priest is, anyway? (Ram-Kee-Pawal-Dadoo-Pantee-Nagar, an 1894 participant in Barnum & Bailey's Ethnological Congress, speaking through a translator, cited in Monsanto 1992:22)

their more limited experience in several African countries, where they have had meetings with presidents, obas, and other high officials, has been similar. Later, when Smithsonian staff members ask them how they liked the tour, they smile graciously and say it was very interesting.

There had been much hoopla about the staff group photo at 9:30, but since the White House tour was scheduled at the same time, our group wasn't in it. Today, rather than communicating last minute changes verbally, xeroxes of the day's schedules, with boxes crossed out and reannotated, are distributed at the presenters' meeting in the Council House. It makes sense; the original sheets we had been working with have become more and more obsolete as the days progress. Today the main stage didn't open till noon, apparently a precedent-setting change for the rest of the Festival.

Sally did an hour of patchwork for children with Aliseti again, and had responsibility for the foodways project; in the afternoon she was slated for a discussion of "Women in Maroon Cultures" and another on "Personal Styles in Dress and Ornament" in the Council House. Rich was to introduce a music and dance program by the Eastern Maroons, participate in a "cross program workshop" on protocol on the narrative stage, and interpret Saramaka folktales for an hour on the main stage.

Fig. 12 On the main stage at the end of a long day—Rich translates as the Saramakas tell tales. Left to right: Djangili, Aduengi, the four women, and Awagi. *Photo by Rebecca Bateman*

The two Guiana troupes have been protesting about the high number of hours they have to dance; the Festival staff expressed sympathy and said they would try to reduce the load. But today, with the main stage operating noon to 5:30, the revised schedule still has them performing on it a full three and a quarter hours. It's hardly surprising if they're usually too exhausted at the end of the day to participate in the after-dinner dance parties that other groups attend in the hotel dining room.

In the generic house, Awagi asserts his authority. "Who put up this sign about no photos?" he asks accusingly. We explain he was absent when the group decided they didn't like being stared at through lenses all the time. Angry, he pulls the sign down, saying that these things are supposed to be discussed with him and that he certainly doesn't want the Saramakas doing anything that could be interpreted as uncooperative toward their hosts.

Meanwhile, Gaamá Songo calls Rich over to vent some anger. He's still fuming about how the chiefs were treated "like dogs" in the White House.

Yesterday the organizers handed Rich a twenty-page stapled packet of pages about the "cross progam workshop" he is responsible for moderating today—a 45-minute program called "Codes of Behavior: Protocol/Comportment." Written by an official Smithsonian coordinator and assistant coordinator of these special programs, it exemplifies the bureaucratic potential of Festivalese. It explains that "the purpose of cross programming is to bring together participants from the different programs to explore connections between their individual experiences and traditions," and that "cross program workshops also provide an opportunity to address cultural issues that cut across programs and cultures." After such introductory generalizations, the document describes the particular workshop in question, which is to feature protocol among Maroons (Colonel Wright and Gaanman Gazon), in the White House (Chief Butler Alonzo Fields and Police Inspector Kenneth Burke), and in Taos Pueblo (Governor Mike Concha) and includes "biographies" of the participants—two to three lines for each of the Maroon chiefs and ten to eleven for each of the U.S. participants.

In a brief meeting with Ken and Diana last night, Rich had admitted that he found the intellectual justification for this event a bit thin, and they had asked Olivia Cadaval (the official coordinator for cross program workshops) to come over to our table to help explain the idea behind these sessions. Rich said he couldn't quite envision how a 45-minute session (which included introductions, ongoing translations between Ndjuka and English, and a dialogue with the audience) could allow all five participants to describe the importance of protocol in their respective realms, demonstrate it through examples, and then engage in a comparative discussion. Olivia protested that she was sure it could be done, if only he were willing to try. Unpersuaded, Rich said he would feel more comfortable if he could simply translate as necessary, while *she* moderated. That way, she could show him what the Festival had in mind for such events. As a result of the discussion, Olivia removed Colonel Wright and Kenneth Burke from the program, leaving Chief Gazon, Alonzo Fields, and Mike Concha, and asked Peter Seitel to serve as master of ceremonies.

After a brief opening about the universality of protocol and the introduction of the participants, Peter asked Concha to talk about what the Governor of Taos does. Concha's reply stressed that he governs with the help of his officers and never makes decisions alone. He also described how the governor and war chief are chosen by the elders in the sacred kiva, and how the governor's role is internal—to take care of the people as well as visitors and tourists within the pueblo. The elderly Alonzo Fields then went on for a good while, using tales he had clearly told many a time, about how he had served meals to various presidents (beginning with Herbert Hoover) and their royal guests, how he had been caught in the middle whenever Franklin and Eleanor disagreed about menus, and so forth—quite entertaining. When Gaanman Gazon was asked by Peter, through Rich, how *he* governed, he told Rich it was "just like the other man [Concha] said," and turned to the microphone to describe the ways chiefs are chosen and how he governs with the help of other officials, before launching into a discussion of the workings of justice in adultery cases.

Whenever the opportunity presented itself, Peter reminded the audience that there were similarities as well as differences in protocol around the world, almost as if to a sixth-grade social studies class. But in spite of Peter's good humor and unflappability, Rich found the ses-

> "Life and death, birth, survival, the life after death, power. . . . Whether you live in Manhattan," Mrs. Vogel said, "and are hassled by the giant corporation you work for, or you live in Mali and worry about insects and the drought killing your crops, the gut issues are the same: wealth and health and survival." (McGill 1984)

sion banal. And ultimately, perhaps, demeaning (despite the intent of honoring the participants) to three dignified men who had very special life experiences which just couldn't begin to be shared in that kind of time, in that kind of setting. And what an irony to be politely discussing protocol right after the *gaanmans'* experience at the White House!

At dinner, Patricia makes a formal request to Sally to write out a list of all the (first) names of the U.S. presidents and their wives, so she can give them to the rest of the children she plans to have. Sally inquires how many she wants. "Sister-in-law," replies Patricia, "I'll need at least twelve."

Around nine o'clock, most of the Suriname group is climbing into their beds, though Akumayai and a couple of others decide to catch the party in the grand ballroom. Suddenly the whole hotel is pierced by the fire alarm. Hidden but powerful loud speakers in the ceilings urge people to walk, not run, to the nearest exits. We race out of our room to alert the Maroons on our floor. The Saramakas understand that there's an emergency, but are nevertheless reluctant to leave, or at least confused about whether that's what to do. They're concerned about being (and being ridiculed as) inexperienced travelers. What do sophisticated travelers do in a hotel fire? They're in their night clothes. And besides, all their possessions would be there in an unattended hotel if everyone left. Couldn't a thief come in and steal everything? If there's a fire everything will go up in smoke. There's a great deal of panicky discussion.

Aduengi is particularly intent on protecting his belongings, and we have trouble pulling him away. He's standing next to his bed throwing clothes, apples, toiletries, and travel documents into a giant suitcase, which he insists on dragging behind him when we finally get everyone headed for the stairwell. On the way down, it opens and begins to leave a trail of crumpled clothing; he runs back to re-stuff the valise. Outside in the night, we stand in the parking lot for an hour or so with the collective hotel occupants—hundreds of Maroons, New Mexicans, Native Americans, and Festival presenters, together with business travelers, clandestine lovers, and vacationing tourists—as the Arlington Fire Department conducts its investigation. The Saramaka women have a bad case of the giggles; it is, in fact, a comical sight. But Awagi pulls them into line with stern reprimands: he sees the whole incident as a ritually dangerous moment, as well as a potential stain on the name of Saramakas and of Suriname. He apparently already knew what we learned only later—that one of the Saramaka women, in a playful mood on the way to the dance party, and curious about what that red handle was, had been the one to pull the alarm.

# Down Days

*Tuesday, 30 June*

The first of two "down days," as Festival staff puts it. The tradition-bearers are neither to perform for the masses nor (if we've understood correctly) to get paid their daily allowance. Planned activities include the pan-Maroon summit (at which Rich is to participate) and a shopping trip (for which Sally is to serve as interpreter). First, Rich's report:

My assignment is to participate, as an official translator, in the "Maroon Peoples' Meeting," billed by program organizers as a high point of the Festival for the Maroons themselves—an opportunity for their leaders to meet each other, voice hopes and grievances, and set up contacts that would evolve into lasting relationships. Awareness of their shared historical experiences, until now relegated largely to a scholarly literature generally unavailable to them and their people, will thus be converted into a tool for their own political and ideological lives. (Later in the day a senior Smithsonian staffer, who hadn't attended the meeting, captured something of its intent when he asked me, with a twinkle in his eye: "How'd the Meeting go? Did you witness the birth of the new pan-American Maroon nation?")

It was a day of ceremony and protocol, in the modernistic Ripley International Center several stories under the Mall. Directed by Ken, experienced ethnographer with long-term commitments to Maroons in both Jamaica and the Guianas, the planning for the meeting reflected ethnographic sensitivity to Maroon perspectives. Adiante, who served as emcee and spontaneous interpreter for the whole meeting, did an inspired job.

After the stage, so to speak, was set, with various dignitaries at their places around the large table or on chairs at the room's edge, Awagi opened the meeting with rhythms played on the *apínti* (talking drum)—first prayers and introductions, then a greeting to the chiefs, and an invitation for them to be seated. Ndjuka drummer Da Kelion followed with rhythms officially announcing the meeting, with phrase-by-phrase verbal responses provided by Basia (Assistant Headman) Molly. James Early, a real man-of-words U.S.-style, then offered a hearty speech of welcome, addressing the theme of freedom: "We are called Maroons, but we should be called Freedom-People." He quoted several spirituals and called on "our spirits and gods" of the African heritage. Richard Kurin's welcome was next: "In the first few days of the Festival, your communities have told a story that people generally in this country do not know. In this country we generally believe that freedom and independence began in 1776 with our own Declaration of Independence. We are only wrong by about two hundred and sixty or seventy years. . . . Many people who have come to the Mall, to the Festival, have learned about your achievements and your accomplishments and I think are enriched by it." He talked about how much the Maroons had to teach us, the organizers' hope that the meeting would also produce new opportunities for the various communities' futures, and the great honor of having them present.

Diana and a few others also welcomed the participants, and Ken went around the room, making individual introductions. Besides the twenty-five or so people at the table (the Suriname chiefs and their under-officers, the Jamaica chiefs and theirs, the French Guiana chief and his, Palenquero representatives, Seminole representatives, the mayor of Maripasoula, the heads of Maroon organizations from Colombia, French Guiana, Ecuador, and the Netherlands, and translators), the meeting was attended by various Smithsonian dignitaries and a number of professors from area institutions, plus the drummers and *abeng*-blower.

The chiefs from the Guianas are asked to speak first. Feeling out of their own element, they hem and haw, look about, and indicate that they're not quite sure they have anything to say. Eventually Gazon, the eldest, begins. With Basia Molly providing formal phrase-by-phrase replies, he speaks for a few minutes, offering formal thanks to all: thanks to Ken, thanks to his superiors at the Smithsonian, thanks to all the Americans for inviting them. Gaamá Songo goes next, addressing Basiá Aduengi: engaging in the kind of rhetoric appropriate for such an occasion, he offers greetings, expresses appreciation, and talks about the common heritage of those around the table. He then asks Basiá

Aduengi to sing a song of thanks, a prayer, a greeting—one of the First-Time songs sung by Saramakas on the day they became free two centuries ago. Aduengi sings *"Hóndóó! Bái hóndóó!"* (which, Adiante explains, is in an esoteric ritual language that he can't translate).

The baton is then passed to Colonel Harris, a master of Victorian-style oratory, who eloquently weaves quotes from the classics he must have taught during his years as head of the Moore Town Maroon School into his extemporaneous speech. Adiante translates into Ndjuka, which is very close to Aluku and can also be followed by Saramakas. "Friends and colleagues," the Colonel begins,

> I think it was Joseph Conrad who in his beautiful English prose remarked that the human tongue is an instrument powerful enough to render any ideas conceived by the human intellect. Yet there are instances in which it is but a poor interpreter. This is particularly so when the sentiments to be expressed are deep and fervent. Sometime in last year, I became aware that the day would come when I—this poor, insignificant speck of humanity—would have the honor and the privilege to be with this representative band of men and women, whose illustrious forebears broke, should we say, asunder impossibility, opened the dungeons of despair and defeat, and wrought victories whose memories will last till the end of time. ... Slavery was indeed an abomination. In fact it was the most abominable manifestation of man's inhumanity to man. All the waters in all the oceans on a planet called earth could not wash clean the hands of its perpetrators, who so demeaned the human family. But I think we all remember a very apt expression—from *The Tempest*, I think—"Let us not burden our remembrances with a heaviness that is past." We, as our ancestors did, can show the world that difficulties should be used as stepping stones to the very acme of success.... We the Maroons . . . are possessors of a unique heritage. Though numerically we are almost inconsequential in the spectrum of earth's teeming millions, the odds we overcame, the historical chapters of surpassing beauty that have been produced by our ancestors, our fathers, our deep fellowship and communion with nature, and our God-given competence where survival is concerned, our genuine love for all men and women of good will—are all testimonies to the fact that we have lit a candle in this at-times dreary world.

Much of Colonel Harris's speech defies simultaneous translation, but Adi rises to the challenge, filling the gaps with appropriate remarks and in general keeping the flavor of the undertaking intact. Meanwhile, Chief Songo leans over to me to ask in a whisper when it will be time for lunch.

Now it's Chief Adochini's turn. Addressing Adiante as yea-sayer, he asks Gazon if he can borrow the Ndjuka *basia* as his formal yea-sayer, since the Aluku who would have served in that role has a cold and can't talk. Gazon agrees. Adochini makes a speech about conducting the meeting with proper respect for all, and expresses gratitude to all those responsible for making this event possible, from Ken and Diana to the president of the United States. Colonel Wright then offers greetings on behalf of the Accompong Maroons, as Colonel Harris (oratorically a very hard act to follow) looks on in apparent disapproval at Wright's less polished speech style. He then goes on to talk about the need for solidarity among oppressed peoples and asks those in attendance not to forget those South Africans who are still in bondage, "our brothers and sisters still under slavery."

Mrs. Charles Wilson of the Seminoles spoke in her no-nonsense, down-home way: "We are just glad to be here . . . so proud to be here, that we are just really overwhelmed. I agree with all of the statements of getting together and coming in as one." After thanking Ian Hancock, Ken, and Diana for giving us "the privilege of meeting our brothers and our sisters," she noted that

> we're all one even though we don't speak the same languages . . . we'll have to learn to, or just wave or smile or something, but to show our gratitude towards you. We're extremely glad to be here. . . . In the behalf of the United States of America, and I *mean* that—white, black, blue, green, but especially our little community over there of the Seminole Indian Scouts—we're just glad to know that you're down here. You make us feel that we *are* somebody. And we hope that you will feel the same toward us.

Then on to the representative from Colombia, Gabino Hernández Palomino, who offered greetings in Spanish and declared that this is a very important meeting for Maroons throughout the Americas—especially to discuss the events surrounding the Quincentenary. There ought to be social reparations from the European nations on that occasion, destined for the Maroons of Latin America, he proposed. And no Maroon should celebrate the Quincentenary, because that would be tantamount to celebrating slavery itself. The 500th should instead be a moment to reflect on the past in terms of the future.

Juan García, the only Ecuadorian present, spoke next, also in

Spanish, saying (in summary): I am here to represent a group of Maroons that is among the least known in the Americas, not because it hasn't been important in Maroon history but because of isolation imposed from without. It's not in the interests of the dominant culture to encourage the study of Maroon culture, so we Maroons must do it for ourselves. Until twenty years ago, there was no general consensus or knowledge about Maroons as a category, the history was preserved only in certain archives or in the collective memory of Maroon communities. . . . [Then, with a definite edge:] We hope that within ten more years we'll know about *all* of the chiefs, even those from little-known places. Thanks to the Smithsonian for inviting us here.

André Pakosie, a Ndjuka who lives in Utrecht, read a very long formal address that he had prepared in English, on behalf of Maroons in the Netherlands; it included a good bit of potted history, some information about Maroon and Amerindian organizations in the Netherlands, and brief allusion to the current civil war. Because it quickly became apparent that his accent and phrasing would make the translating task even more difficult than it had been for Colonel Harris, Adi asked whether he could wait and try to summarize the gist of it at the end; in fact, Ken stepped in as soon as Pakosie had read a closing poem to change the subject and ask for comments from others present.

Abienso, the Mayor of the French Guiana *commune* of Maripasoula, made a two-minute speech in English, proposing politely that this meeting was only a beginning. Songo leans over to me again, this time to ask when the group photo will be taken. There has, by this time, been some mention of *apinti* rhythms being played before the group breaks for lunch; Chief Songo reminds me, whispering, of a firm rule of Saramaka council etiquette: "Friend, don't let them play the *apinti* when we get up for lunch; if they do that we can't sit down at the meeting again." I transmit the message to Ken, who consults Gazon, and a decision is taken not to play the *apinti* until the end of the whole meeting. The floor opens up for general discussion, but no one seems to have anything to say, despite repeated pleas from the organizers, one of whom looks distinctly distressed. We break for lunch a bit early.

The midday meal, specially arranged by Ken and catered by a Mrs. Brown (who runs a Jamaican bakery in Baltimore), was a high point of the event. The Suriname participants quickly labelled it the best meal of the Festival, one remarking with feeling, "Finally, we're eating real Suriname food!"

We are called back to the meeting room by Jamaican drumming and *abeng*-playing. Three minutes standing followed by three sitting. The *gaanman*s are asked by Diana to say something about their common problems: economic development, the exodus of Maroon children out of Maroon territories, the status of treaties, the possibilities for a respectful kind of tourism. Gazon cooperatively takes the floor, inquiring what country it is that just played the *abeng*. Someone says Jamaica. "We Ndjukas have it, too," notes Gazon. "It talks. . . . The *apinti* also talks. . . . But our own people don't really know it anymore."

It's Songo's turn and he obediently poses the questions that District Commissioner Libretto has instructed him during the lunch break to ask: Who owns the land where the Jamaicans live, and who owned the country? Colonel Harris answers with a brief history of the treaties and the status of communal lands, specifying that the country was owned first by the Spanish, then the British. Libretto evokes the problems that can arise when the national government grants concessions for goldmining or other purposes on Maroon lands, and inquires whether anything like that has happened in Jamaica. Harris cites a turn-of-the-century case in which the colonial government wanted to build a road through Maroon territory, but the Maroons were able to prevent it. Palomino, from Colombia, chimes in with some comparative material. In 1958, he explains, a law was passed saying that lands occupied by Maroons and other Blacks, particularly on the Pacific coast, belonged to the state. So, unlike Amerindians, Blacks have no land of their own in Colombia. He expresses the hope that some general principles useful to all Maroons can come out of this meeting.

Throughout, Libretto carefully stage-manages the Suriname chiefs. Gazon, following his instructions, offers a brief history of Ndjuka officialdom and tells how there are now female village officials in Suriname (though only at relatively low rank), asking about the status of women in public life elsewhere. The Colombians say that although in slave times black women were considered important only for their reproductive potential, they are now struggling to be on a par with men. Colonel Wright from Accompong comments that women are very active in church services and teaching, and cites Indira Gandhi as a role model. "Also in other countries, women have been playing great roles. Women have great value as people, and without them—you couldn't do without them. So, let's . . . let them do what they want to do. Don't stifle them, 'cause it's they who brought us here and we must pay a great respect to them." In answer to a question from the Surinamers, Colonel Wright invokes the story of the Jamaican national hero Nanny, the great leader of the eastern Maroons during their wars of liberation.

Adochini, who doesn't have a district commissioner looking over his shoulder since he's from French Guiana, speaks more forthrightly than the others about land rights: We don't have rights like the Saramakas and Ndjukas, he declares; the French government simply takes our land. Colonel Harris takes the floor for a semantic footnote, suggesting that he may have misspoken himself in talking earlier about "communal" land, since he did not mean to imply that people were free to do anything they wanted on land being used by someone else. Colonels Harris and Wright have a testy, whispered internecine squabble, much to the amusement of the Suriname chiefs. Adochini goes on for some time, explaining how Alukus are now struggling to wrest some control from the French over their lands and he ends by requesting support from everyone present.

A member of the Seminole group brings the discussion back to the role of women as leaders, pointing out that Mrs. Wilson, present at the meeting, is—by dint of age and experience—their "premier representative," and that their current president is also "a lady." Palomino then offers some ethnography about *cuadros* and women's lives in Palenque, invoking the African heritage. Major Charles Aarons of the Moore Town Maroons, suggesting that all the Maroon communities represented are "still enjoying the penalties of slavery," proposes asking the various governments that signed the historic treaties to recognize and acknowledge them.

Adochini veers back to the issue of women, which Libretto had endorsed at the lunch table as a particularly appropriate subject to discuss this afternoon. The exchange is semi-staged. Among the Aluku, says Adochini, a woman could never be captain or chief, she could only be an assistant headman. Libretto: Why? Adochini: Because they have so many *kina* [taboos]. Libretto: You mean menstrual taboos. Songo breaks in to comment that *basiá* work isn't as serious as captain's work, which is why women can be *basiá* but not captain. Colonel Harris makes a gracious disclaimer that he in no way wishes to interfere in the internal affairs of another community, but only to speak honestly and openly and constructively among brothers and sisters and friends. After citing in extenso the Christian hymn "Once to every man and nation," and stressing the verse that runs "time makes ancient good uncouth," he alludes delicately to "the days when those rules were brought into vogue" and how they served their purpose at the time. But now, he argues, when we're living almost in the twenty-first century, many of the taboos we had against women are not good enough for our times. The women have proved themselves in all our communities. . . . Adi's translation renders the colonel's long speech with diplomacy, skipping over the specifics and generalizing that it was important for communities to respect their women—thus avoiding any conflict of ideologies, or any kind of cross-cultural dialogue at all.

Abienso goes back to land rights, asserting that the French have tricked the Aluku. He would like to have a piece of paper to prove ownership of each piece of their territory. The major problem is that all rights have been oral. And he is concerned that this seems true of all the Maroon communities present today. Colonel Harris discusses the situation in Moore Town, legislated by themselves for themselves: land can be bought and sold but only within the Maroon community. Colonel Wright stresses the importance of not selling land to outsiders, but keeping it for future generations. Farika Birhan, an Accompong activist who lives in the U.S., describes at length some of her international efforts on behalf of education and the preservation of Maroon culture in Jamaica. As the discussion gradually loses steam, Pakosie describes a meeting he had with President Venetiaan of Suriname about Maroon land rights, and proposes that everyone at the present meeting exchange addresses so they can contact each other and the Smithsonian can bring everyone together again. Diana offers some closing remarks on behalf of the Smithsonian, which Ken renders in Aluku. Then, at a signal from Ken, the drumming starts up, this time by Papa Baala of the Alukus, and the meeting ends with appropriate ceremony.

Meanwhile, Sally's been shopping:

For the trip, participants have been told that the buses will leave at 9:00 A.M. Travel to the mall takes twenty minutes, but the stores don't open till 10:00. As the group stands around waiting for the mall to open, I can't help but marvel at the planning.

Before the trip got started, the Ndjuka women were very unhappy because Linda Lenoir, a native speaker of Paramaka (an Eastern Maroon language very close to Ndjuka), was kept at the hotel to take care of Samakon, who has been in the emergency room of the hospital, and who may have to be flown back to Suriname. My Saramaccan filled the breach, however, and the Ndjuka and Saramaka women, plus Djangili, toured the mall as a group, eventually buying shoes, rice pots, thermos boxes, yarn, thread, skin creams, and toothpaste.

There was a little trouble in the discount shoe outlet where the clerk reacted with fear and eventually outright hostility, as this strange group spread out through the aisles, pulling out boxes and gesticulating with questions she couldn't understand. In a more upscale department store, however, the chic woman selling French perfumes gladly offered sample sprays; in contrast to the rainforest scents in The Body Shop, Chanel and Guerlain elicited excited approval from the Saramakas, and then disappointment as the price tags were revealed.

No Spanish interpreter had been assigned to the trip, but the Palenqueros managed pretty well, tracking me down from time to time when they couldn't communicate with a clerk. Coming back to the bus at the prearranged time, we discovered that Marilyn Abel, the staff person who had organized the outing, had been rushed back to the hotel with an emergency illness, which left the bus driver and me in charge of seeing that all fifty tradition-bearers were present and accounted for.

Back at the Marriott. White bread, salad, and cold cuts for lunch. No rice. Saramaka women pile up their plates with slices of bread since they don't like uncooked vegetables or cold meat.

Many of the Maroons have been asking what they're supposed to do about laundry, so we locate the hotel's facility and assemble dirty clothes and lots of quarters—yet another aspect of life in the U.S. to help them explore. The small room, lined with washers, dryers, and detergent dispensing machines, is hot, noisy, and filled with Festival participants either processing their laundry or waiting in line for a free machine. Coming back several times over the course of the evening, we finally find a lull and manage to get the clothes washed, dried, and redistributed to their owners.

In the evening in the lobby, the two of us bump into Diana and Ken, who mention that since the Maroons have already had a shopping day, it will be the other groups' turn to go tomorrow. We protest and point out that the literature we had been given announced a Wednesday shopping spree especially for the Maroons since some of them had been in the Tuesday meeting; on the basis of that written directive, we say, we had promised the performers a Wednesday shopping trip, and we don't feel we can go back on that. They have been counting on having Wednesday to shop, and it means a lot to them. Diana looks distressed, Ken disgruntled. There are too many people to fit in the one bus that's available, they say. But they generously agree to try to work something out. They have enough vans, they say, but there aren't any drivers. Rich offers to drive. So that's where it's left, tentatively.

This particular logistical problem was just one out of the hundreds that Ken and Diana have had to solve on any given day. They're both working in double overdrive to make the Maroon Program a success, not sleeping more than a few hours a night and constantly doing their best to be in seventeen different places at once.

*Wednesday, 1 July*

The second "down day." Adi has, with great effort and determination, worked out arrangements for several of the Maroons to attend an Orioles game (free tickets and seating in a VIP box, transportation, and at least a minimal orientation so they'll understand what's happening). Djangili shows up in the lobby all outfitted in a suit and flashy tie, ready for the expedition. Looking very pleased with himself, he comments to Sally that he's wearing a *pikí miíi síki* ("little children's disease"). The word-play follows a familiar polyglot logic, but it still takes her a few seconds to fit the pieces together; although the Saramaccan word for suit jacket is *djákiti*, the Dutch word is *jas*, which Saramakas pronounce the same as their term for yaws (*jási*).

Ken and Diana have arranged to give us the use of a van to take Saramakas shopping, despite angry Ndjuka protests that they're not being hosted as well as the Saramakas. We've made a list of what they would like to buy: Gaamá Songo wants several felt hats; others are looking for tape recorders, radios, and batteries of various specifications; a few want watches; we have requests for bath towels (which women sometimes wear as skirts back home); and so forth. With Diana's assistance we've planned out an itinerary that touches all the desired bases: Circuit City, Bed and Bath, J. C. Penney, Sears.

The shopping is conducted under real time pressure, with each of us trying to help in as many of the diverse commercial exchanges as we can. In Circuit City things become particularly hectic as a slew of radios, tape recorders, and batteries are chosen, brought from the stockroom, and paid for out of the several different coin purses and envelopes stuffed with U.S. dollars that each person has brought, representing pre-paid requests from relatives in their home villages.

With a strict deadline for the return of the van, the squeeze was really on when we finally got to the Sears watch department. The single clerk was barraged by diverse requests, since each person was looking for a different model. As Sally urged people back to the van, Rich took an extra few minutes to help Songo choose a gold watch befitting his status. On the way out, Songo finally spotted just the kind of felt hat he had been looking for. But he still needed shoes, and as we raced back to return the van all of them were talking about the things they hadn't had time to buy.

After lunch at the hotel, we suggested a trip on the metro to the Museum of African Art, and set off with five or six members of the group. The long escalators down into the tunnels, the cavernous stations we glided through, and the passengers who recognized them from their performances on the Mall provided great excitement. Djangili was already taking careful note of the features of particular stations we passed through and making plans to re-do the trip on his own. Compared to the metro ride, the museum was a distinct anti-climax; as they did the walk-through, they were already talking with anticipation about some residual shopping in the warren of underground stores we had passed at the Rosslyn metro entrance. In a drugstore, some found toothpaste and others hair products; Patricia took Sally aside to ask where she could find "*sekisi búku*" (porn mags) to take back, but we couldn't locate any.

Over the past day or two, the Festival organizers' oft-stated goal of encouraging personal exchange among the members of different groups during their off-hours has backfired in an unexpected way. Maroons, sharing their experiences with participants from New Mexico around the large round dinner tables, have uncovered an aspect of the events' organization that had until then remained a discreetly guarded secret: a significant gap in the amount of money they're getting paid. As their full compensation for participation in the Festival, each Maroon is receiving $27 a day; New Mexicans, like all the presenters, are getting $90. This discrepancy constitutes a hidden undercurrent of difference at the Festival that, for understandable if not very noble reasons, none of the participants have been invited to know about. When the news got out and Festival organizers were asked to explain it, they cited a visa-based restriction for non-U.S. participants who weren't classified as professional performers. The issue led to a number of heated discussions with Festival staff—both by Maroons, who interpreted it as discrimination, and by the two of us, who wondered whether it didn't reflect a slipshod and ungenerous handling of the available visa options.

The issue constituted a stress point at which the ideology and public discourse of fun and togetherness locked horns with the practical realities of putting on a magnum-size cultural happening. The organizers' replies to the rumbling dissatisfaction followed two lines: first, that it wasn't possible to pay the Maroons more because of visa restrictions, and second that the whole point of the Festival was personal and cultural enrichment, not monetary gain. As one of them expressed it to us, "We would hope that togetherness and self-discovery could compensate for the fact that we aren't in a position to pay more than pocket money." At the base of the disagreement is the ques-

[On World's Fair, St. Louis, stationery:] October 22, 1903—Sir: By authority of the Louisiana Purchase Exposition Company, you are hereby commissioned as a Special Agent of this Department, and authorized to organize and conduct an expedition into the interior of Africa for the purpose of obtaining anthropological material and *offering certain natives* [another letter specified twelve pygmies and, "if practicable, King Ndombe of the Bikenge"] *the opportunity of attending the Exposition in person.* I have the honor to be, Yours with respect, [signed] W J McGee, Chief [of the Department of Anthropology]. (Bradford and Blume 1992:240–41, our italics)

[When the exhibiting of a large contingent of Filipinos was proposed for the early-twentieth century Portland fair,] rather than paying the Filipinos, Felder [the organizer] proposed putting the money into the improvement of trails in the appropriate provinces in the islands. (Rydell 1984:194)

tion of whether participants are being offered an exciting opportunity to see the world or have been brought in to do skilled work. The answer, of course, is both.

Saramakas were quick to read the practice and its rationalizations as discrimination against them. Kayanasii remarked that the Festival organizers were taking Saramakas for *káu*; but we're not dumb like cows, she said, and we understand exactly what they're doing. (Later a Maroon studying for his Ph.D. in Holland, who had flown in for the Festival, made a point of distinguishing Gaamá Songo's objection to being treated like "dogs" at the White House from the more recently developed complaint that they were being treated like "cows." The term *dágu*, he pointed out, denotes ordinariness and lack of distinction, but *káu* suggests brute stupidity.) Furthermore, the Saramakas argued, they could easily have been issued visas as professional performers; in fact, that's the only way they ever traveled. In order to

It is essential to emphasize that, whether performing or demonstrating, participants felt they were putting their reputations on the line. (Bauman et al. 1992:50)

prove the point, Awagi rummaged through his carry-on bag and found a 1985 certificate attesting that he had been awarded the Suriname government's Gold Medal of Honor for cultural diplomacy, together with his typed C.V., which listed twenty-three professional performing trips, to Grenada, the Netherlands, Trinidad and Tobago, Guyana, Nigeria, Cuba, Barbados, Curaçao, French Guiana, Germany, and Ghana, as well as Los Angeles, New York, Baltimore, and even Washington D.C. Those tours had involved a limited set of performances, he emphasized, rather than morning-to-evening responsibilities, and he had always been correctly compensated for his specialized skills. Similarly, Djangili cited the various advanced courses in modern dance that he had paid to attend in Paramaribo over the years, and the diplomas and certificates of merit he had been awarded as a result. Akumayai brought up her recent trip to Pomona, California, where she had been paid a thousand dollars for just a few appearances on stage. And one of the Alukus described a recent trip to Holland, France, Germany, and Switzerland, for which each performer received a total of about $2000—230 francs per day for the whole period of travel, though they didn't perform each day.

The group requested a meeting with the organizers of the Maroon Program, and were granted a late evening appointment in the hotel lobby, where they pleaded their case. We've been working very hard every day, they argued, throwing all our energy into each activity. And

> There was the ongoing story of the Zulus [at St. Louis, 1904]. A St. Louis promoter had come up with the idea of recreating the decisive battle of the Boer War twice daily on the Pike. General Piet Cronje, the Boer commander, many of his regulars, and many of the British troops who defeated him at the Modder River in South Africa in 1900 were brought to St. Louis. To provide authentic background . . . a hundred Zulus were induced to come as well. The Boers and the British were local favorites, wined and dined throughout the city, but the Zulus were never paid the four dollars a week they had been promised. They began to rebel. (Bradford and Blume 1992:114)

that's what we intend to keep doing. We're serious about our work and about honoring our commitments to the letter; it's important to us to uphold the reputation that Saramakas have in the world. Given all that, we would like you to explore the possibility of increasing what we are paid—if only as a gesture of your appreciation for the kind of contribution we are making to the Festival.

The Alukus expressed preference for a different solution to the problem. We've understood from the first that you can't pay us more, they said, but we hadn't understood that we would be asked to work so hard, for so many hours a day. Pay us at $27 a day, but please couldn't you reduce our workload?

> The reframing of folk culture by high cultural institutions can for festival participants be deeply confusing and potentially

> painful. . . . [Some] struggled with the question of their own role—
> were they guests, hirelings, or honorees? In ways seldom ac-
> knowledged by public folklife presenters, most of the participants
> came with well-developed and fully articulated political and
> personal aims: to wield political influence in some area of impor-
> tance, to expand a clientele, to accomplish a specific project of
> work, or simply—and perhaps most tellingly—to earn some
> money. (Cantwell 1992:265–66)

The first such meeting ended without a resolution; Saramakas requested a follow-up. It was held late the next night, and although we were not invited to be present, Djangili reported back to us on its tone and conclusion. The organizers cited the high cost of the group's air

> The remuneration of these people, in addition to their board and
> travelling expenses, is usually nominal. I shall see that they are
> presented with fancy articles such as are always acceptable and a
> small allowance monthly. . . . I must study economy, inasmuch as I
> propose to add this "Congress of Nations" to the other attractions
> of our great show without extra charge. (From an 1882 letter,
> apparently sent to some two hundred U.S. diplomats and other
> representatives living abroad, by P. T. Barnum, as part of his
> efforts to "form a collection, in pairs or otherwise, of all the
> uncivilized races in existence," cited in Monsanto 1992:15–16)

fare and lodging, explained once again that the visas carried restrictions on compensation, alluded to the limitations of the Festival budget, said the work load wouldn't have been so heavy if the Mexican participants had shown up as planned, expressed sympathy and concern for the Maroon position, and apologized that there wasn't more money. Djangili, who had been designated spokesperson for the Saramakas (Songo would have been demeaned by even being present at such a discussion), countered that he wasn't really interested in listening to all the reasons and constraints and feelings of solidarity; all he wanted to know was the verdict, yes or no. Had they been able to find a way to give them a little extra money? His point finally got through after several tries, and the organizers had to admit that they hadn't. The Saramakas said good night politely and left.

We've been thinking about the logic of personal and cultural enrichment. If that's compensation enough to justify the participation of Saramakas, why wouldn't it also be sufficient to justify the participation of other "tradition-bearers"? If everyone—including presenters—

had been given $27/day (which might better, it seems to us, have been paid for the entire trip rather than just the nine official "working days"), the issue would simply have been chalked up to the non-profit nature of the Festival. It was the gap between two different kinds of tradition-bearers that caused the outrage. Their titles, their status, their accomodations, and their duties were defined in identical terms; indeed, with responsibility for five stages/areas each, the 62-member Maroon delegation ended up with a more exhausting schedule than the 106-person New Mexican delegation. But the money in their pockets was off by a factor of more than three.

A second bone of contention has been the timing of the disbursements. Although participants received a small portion during the first week, the remainder isn't to be paid until the end of the Festival, when all available shopping time has expired. The organizers explain to us that the reason for paying on the last day is that the Maroons will then have some money to take back home with them. But wait a minute: Even if that were what the Maroons wished, this reasoning suggests that they wouldn't have the self-control to hold onto the money if it were given to them earlier. In fact, the Saramakas very much wanted the money as early as possible so that they could take advantage of the same discount-price consumer opportunities that people from every country in the Americas come to the United States for. One of the staffers suggests, not very helpfully, that they can find things to spend their money on in the souvenir shops at the Miami airport. . . .

In the end, it turns out that this aspect of Festival plans cannot be changed. Nor can the proceeds from the crafts each participant has left on consignment be distributed any earlier than the eve of their morning departure from the U.S. On a more positive note, however, a decision has been made to make payments in cash rather than checks, after we argued that even those Maroons with enough experience to deal with a U.S. bank teller have been left no time to *go* to a bank.

# On the Mall, Again

*Thursday, 2 July*

Tonight is the much publicized Special Event: the *Booko Dei*, billed as "An evening of Maroon ceremonial drumming and dance from Suriname and French Guiana, South America," and intended more generally (according to a statement by the program organizers) "to commemorate collectively those African Americans who died fighting for freedom."

At 8:30 A.M., the Saramaka women are singing a *sêkêti* song they've just made up: *Déé Améika / De tá pêè kôni ku mi ku môni-o / Háti u mi boónu, déé sèmbè / Mi kê gó u mi-éé*. ("Those Americans / They're playing around with me over money / I'm feeling angry, folks / I want to get myself out of here.")

9:00 A.M. meeting of Ndjukas, Alukus, and Saramakas at The Site. An announcement is made by Djangili: "The bosses have given us an answer. Nothing can be changed. They can't get any more money. So let's accept that graciously and all work together. We can't let Suriname's reputation be spoiled." To the Saramakas, the only thing that's at stake now is reputation.

10:00 A.M. meeting of the staff and presenters. The heads of the program announce that a revised schedule for today will be passed out at the end of the meeting; that means we will see it only a few minutes before the space opens to the public, when all the presenters and performers are supposed to know what they're doing. They remind us that opening ceremonies for the Booko Dei will be held at 5:30, and that the main event will start at 7:00.

A question is posed: If the Booko Dei begins as soon as the daily program ends, when will the performers have a chance to go back to the hotel to shower and get dressed? Maroons have made clear, even in their summary Council House presentations of "Personal Style in Dress and Ornament," that the leisurely process of bathing, rubbing on lotions and perfumes, doing one's hair, and dressing in special clothes

> Many [participants in the 1985 FAF] found their personal needs,
> such as an opportunity to clean up for an evening reception after a
> day in the sun, neglected, and occasionally experienced the habits
> of other participants, from other cultural groups, as grossly
> discourteous or intrusive. . . . On the whole, it seems, folk festivals
> have occurred in an intellectual tradition that cannot wholly credit
> the human competence of the participant nor thoroughly conceive
> his or her fundamental cultural difference. (Cantwell 1992:266)

and accessories is the required beginning of any such event. As Songo
declared flatly, "People don't do funerals without bathing."

Ken proposes that not everyone will have to be involved at 5:30, so
the others can go back to the hotel for a few minutes if they want. We
point out that *everyone* needs a breather and a chance to dress. And
what about dinner? Again, the plan is for everyone to eat more or less
when they can catch time for a box lunch. The manager of the main
stage, Hélène Monteil, makes a plea that they need a break. Sally
seconds her: without a real break it's a 9:00 A.M. to 1:00 A.M. work day:
sixteen hours. Even without worrying about the pledge a few days ago
to cut down on the performers' load, isn't that a bit much? The
program heads suggest putting it to a vote. All the Maroon presenters
seem to favor a break, and a decision is taken to close the Festival at
four so the tradition-bearers can go back and freshen up.

Sally's schedule has red boxes around three Council House events—
a Cross-Program (Pan-Festival) Workshop on "Façades and House Dressing," a discussion of "Women in Maroon Cultures," and another on
"Personal Style in Dress & Ornament"—plus two programs on the
main stage, "Saramaka Music and Dance" and "Maroon Story Songs."
Rich has been assigned two Eastern Maroon dance programs on the
main stage, a 75-minute session on "Traditions of Self Government" in
the Council House, and the culinary preparations for the Booko Dei.
We both have red boxes around the evening's Special Event. In the
course of the meeting, adjustments are made; Sally is excused from her
second Council House program after she points out that she's scheduled to be on the main dance stage at the same time, and the plan for
Maroons to prepare the Booko Dei food offerings is abandoned in
deference to their heavy schedule on the stages of the dance, narrative,
and activities areas (a total of eight hours).

The Saramakas are becoming increasingly concerned about the sale of the crafts that they have deposited in the Museum Shop. Most mornings, a couple of men go over before the gates open to see how things are moving. Adiante helps them adjust prices downward as necessary; they're determined not to take anything back to Suriname once they've gone to the trouble of transporting it to Washington. And they see these sales as an important opportunity to get some cash.

Songo hasn't yet been able to buy shoes, and we have no time free to take him shopping again. But Gary Brana-Shute, a State Department anthropologist who did work with urban Surinamers, volunteers to go with him, much to Songo's delight. Numerous other kindnesses are being provided by people with ties to Suriname who aren't on duty as presenters, and this is especially important for the Alukus and Ndjukas since all three active presenters for the Aluku-Ndjuka-Saramaka contingent (Adiante and the two of us) are Saramaka-focused. (District Commissioner Libretto was, partly for bureaucratic reasons, designated as a presenter, but isn't really functioning in that role.) John Lenoir, who had done anthropological work with Paramakas before becoming an attorney, has helped out in many small ways; his daughter Linda, whose mother is Paramaka, is playing a central role for the Eastern Maroons and they've developed real affection for her. Shelby Givens, who wrote a dissertation on the Aluku, has also helped, and took a memorable stroll across the bridge to Georgetown with three Alukus, which he's writing up for the *Washington Post* (see Givens 1992). The Ndjukas have enjoyed the presence of Janina Rubinowitz, an old friend of Gaanman Gazon, over a couple of days. And Naomi Glock, a missionary-linguist who has spent much of the last twenty years in the Saramaka chief's village, presented an elaborately frosted cake to Songo, who had slices redistributed in the evening to Saramakas throughout the hotel.

We have been told that a golf cart will come by at 11:45 to take the Saramakas to lunch, but when it shows up there's no volunteer available to stand watch over our collective belongings in the generic structure while we're away. During the next half hour, efforts are made to find someone, but without result. Sally, Patricia, and Kayanasii have a Pan-Festival Workshop coming up at 12:45, so they race off to the food tent to queue up and gulp down.

As in the information packet for the cross-program workshop on protocol, the four biographies provided for the house dressing workshop were of different lengths: thirteen and seventeen lines for each of the U.S. participants and a single two-liner for the two Maroons. Perhaps that explains why the person who chaired the session introduced Kayanasii as "Kadjinasay" and announced, erroneously, that the women were from the villages of Dangogo and Asindoopo. To be sure, the correct village names don't matter to a Festival audience on a hot July morning on the Washington Mall. But the pretense of caring about such things annoys Sally enough so that she re-introduces them later with correct names and mentions that they are from the villages of Godo and New Aurora (Tjalikonde). If you don't do your homework, she muses, you can still *look* like you're honoring individuals. But isn't it a charade that in some way has the opposite effect?

During the first half of the program, the Saramaka women came dangerously close to sleep listening to Sally's whispered translations of the adobe expert from New Mexico and the White House stone carver speaking of their respective expertises. After a general summary of Saramaka house decoration and a few questions to the speakers on adobe and stone carving, the program chair announced that the group was going to move en masse to the Guianas area, where festival-goers could talk with the Saramakas in more detail about their house dressing. Although the Saramaka presentation was intended to complement those on adobe and stone carving that the Council House audience had just heard, the rest of the crowd milling about in the Guianas area made communication difficult, especially since the requisitioned microphone did not, in the end, come through. The mandate to combine voice projection, ethnographic interviewing (or rather, prompting), and linguistic and cultural translation in two directions—in an area that was constantly being crisscrossed by uninvolved festival-goers— proved frustrating.

As the days pass, the four Saramaka women feel increasingly reluctant to help out in the Activities Center. (This is the stage on which Saramaka cultural practice is, in watered-down form, made "available" for visitors, particularly young ones, to try for themselves. We wonder about the implications of the appropriation of one people's work routines, religious expression, and creative achievements as another's amusement or recreation.) Three of them consistently beg out of the children's class in making "patchwork textiles" from colored construction paper. Aliseti also pleads that she doesn't want to do it, but comes through each time, and does a wonderful job. In contrast, they all enjoy the cooking, repeatedly opting for complex recipes even when simple ones are in the program. They much prefer "tying *muungá*" (the sweet coconut-rice flour-peanut confection that's wrapped in banana leaves) to "roasting *boón*" (a pancake-like sweet made with flour and sugar)—not just because it's especially good to eat at the end, but also because it has strong associations with festive occasions and they have fun cooking it together. Their greatest frustration is that, with so many tasks assigned to them in the course of the day, they often can't finish the cooking project they've begun in the morning. The day they set out to make peanut rice, for example, they weren't able to find enough time between their scheduled appearances on one stage or another to keep the fire going until it was cooked. It's just too much.

As for fielding questions in the Council House about their lives back home, both the women and the men are explicit that they consider those "narrative stage" sessions at once boring and personally uncomfortable. (At one point, as the sound technician was making pre-program adjustments in the positioning of the speakers' microphones, Kayanasii, feeling irritated, whispered to Sally, "Tell that man to get his penis out of my mouth!")

But they end up doing what is asked of them, and doing it well, frequently taking a couple of minutes ahead of time to plan out some aspect of the presentation. In a discussion of women's lives for which they had been told the audience would be interested in polygyny, for example, someone from the audience posed a question about how women felt toward their husband's other wives; as soon as it was translated, two of the women erupted into a mock fight on stage, lunging at each other and shouting obscenities, as the third attempted futilely to pull them apart and restore peace. And the first time they told folktales, which happened on the narrative stage, the general table of contents had clearly been worked out by Awagi ahead of time.

Another aspect of the planning involves a strong determination to avoid negative images of Saramaka, as part of the notion that they are here in the role of cultural diplomats. Awagi and, to a lesser extent, Djangili have taken on responsibility for overseeing the appropriateness, from a Saramaka perspective, of each presentation. The women received explicit instructions, for example, to lighten the undercurrent of hostility that marks co-wife relations. Their comic enactment of a co-wife fight represented a considered solution to the dilemma of fielding questions about a friction-ridden aspect of social life that they would have preferred not to focus attention on, relegating it to the realm of slapstick and thus removing some of the tension.

As part of their main stage presentation for the day, Saramakas put on a *papá gádu* play—possession dancing for the snake gods. It was as sweet a play as you'd be likely to see on the upper Suriname River. For a few magical moments, the staging all but disappeared and a ritual event sprang to life.

Fig. 13 Saramakas pose with possession-dance regalia. Left to right: Kayanasii, Akumayai, Djangili, Patricia, Aliseti. *Photo by Roland L. Freeman*

Finally it's time for the much touted Booko Dei. The organizers have taken pains to avoid an irresponsible mixture of customs from different Maroon groups, designating the celebration as a specifically Eastern Maroon version. One of them tells us that Johannes Toyo, a young Paramaka Maroon who puts on cultural shows in Paramaribo, is being paid "a couple of hundred dollars" to organize the event. Two women from the Washington community have been hired to handle "outreach" and bring in the crowds. A special flyer has been distributed to announce the day's program:

| | |
|---|---|
| 11:00 A.M. – 5:30 P.M. | Day-time preparations for Booko Dei on the festival site |
| 5:30 P.M. | Drumming, opening libations, and procession to Maroon area. In front of the National Museum of American History, New Mexico tent. |
| 7:00 P.M. – 1:00 A.M. | Booko Dei ceremony, at the Maroon music and dance tent on the Festival site. |

The "opening ceremony," scheduled for 5:30, is held in a tent near the American History Museum. The audience waits patiently until 6:20, when opening rhythms are played by drummers from Suriname and Jamaica. Several people address the large assembly. James Early speaks once again of "this place called Earth," remarking that we cannot determine what the Maroons say but can only assist them in communicating who they are. ("We do not have the power to empower people, but we can assist them. I ask you to participate with respect and humility. . . .") He is followed by Diane Greene (from the National Museum of American History), Richard Kurin ("What we're doing here is not just mere entertainment, not just mere spectacle, . . . but a chance to let these people tell their own stories in their own words"), and Diana N'Diaye (about how the Washington community would like to salute these "freedom fighters," honoring their presence in the capital and the North American continent), plus various Washington dignitaries and Festival sponsors. Then comes an extended blessing of the Booko Dei, conducted on the dance-floor-like platform in front of the stage: a succession of be-robed libation-pourers (mostly African Americans who had gone to Africa to be trained by a traditional priest) declaim prayers in various African languages. There are few smiles; the tone is one of heavy ethnic momentousness.

An introduction to the prayer presented in Twi specifies that there will be an English translation provided "so we can all participate"; the Saramakas, sitting with us on benches in the audience, ask us in whispers when they'll be able to eat. Then an appearance by members of a Yoruba temple in Washington. Diana thanks "all those who have come to honor the specialness of the event." Half an hour after the libations begin, a microphone is brought onstage for the libation pourers. Finally, everyone is invited to "process" to the music stage for the Booko Dei itself.

That introduced a glitch concerning dinner. Instead of processing to the stage, the Maroons followed special instructions to go to the Jamaican area of The Site, where dinner would be waiting. But the group numbered perhaps a hundred, and only thirty-five dinners had been ordered. This produced a mixture of irritation and panic, followed by frantic walkie-talkie orders for more food, and a reduction of the portions, to stretch out the available resources. Staff members were upset because there were too many Maroons asking for box-dinners and none providing the scheduled entertainment; Maroons were frustrated because they were being herded around without getting fed. Tempers were definitely short.

> I feel that in some senses the staff, in its enthusiasm, planned just a little too much. Thursday's events began very early in the day and continued until late at night—and this was after already several days of festival activities. The participants in the Booko Dei ceremony had little time between their activities on the field and the evening events to take a break, wash up and relax. The confusion that resulted from transporting participants back to the hotel in rush hour traffic I felt could have been avoided with altered expectations for what could reasonably be accomplished within the span of the day's activities. While everything eventually worked itself out, the anxiety and stress caused were things that, in a festival environment, everyone could have done without. (Imani Mary Drayton-Hill, Booko Dei Outreach Coordinator, in a report dated 7/20/92)

We finally arrive at the dance tent, which is packed to overflowing; letters and flyers have gone out to a number of community organizations, and word of mouth about the animated dance party several nights ago has swollen the anticipation. Hélène, the stage manager, is at her wits' end; she has been holding the audience for an hour and still no one is ready to perform. And the staffers in charge of the event are nowhere to be found.

About two hours behind schedule, in the midst of total confusion, Djangili decides just to get the thing started. He steps up to the microphone, calls Rich over to translate what he is going to say, and begins to explain what a *día boóko* (Saramakas' term for *booko dei*) is for. But he is soon pulled off the stage by an angry staffer; this is an Eastern Maroon celebration, Johannes Toyo's event, and Toyo is the one who is going to introduce it. Taking note of this, Sally decides she will not approach the microphone that evening unless the organizers ask her to. They don't.

More confusion, more delays, an undercurrent of bickering. Toyo eventually shows up and takes the microphone to begin his prepared introduction. But the audience has become restless, and the spontaneity of the previous evening performance just isn't there, in spite of a program that includes several Eastern Maroon styles—*mato, susa,* and *awasa*—as well as *kawina*. Intergroup resentments of various sorts have surfaced, and the Saramakas, feeling tired and relegated to the margins, ask to go back to the hotel and get some sleep. But the event has been announced for a 1:00 A.M. closing, and they're told that an earlier ride back can't be arranged.

> The display of people is largely about power relationships, though it has other aspects. There is a major difference in status between the exhibitor and the individuals exhibited. The latter give up or have taken away from them certain rights. Sometimes these rights are closely defined by contract as to hours, places, actions to be performed. Sometimes, exhibited individuals lose virtually all their rights. (Benedict 1983:43)

During the long evening, Hélène receives word that a close friend has died of breast cancer. After a good cry in the staff trailer, she dries her eyes and attempts to resume her duties. She asks Sally whether the Saramakas (who have seen her crying and expressed their sympathy) would be willing to dedicate one of their performance numbers to the memory of her friend. Aduengi suggests that this evening isn't the appropriate moment, but that they will do it tomorrow.

The packed house thins out steadily as the Eastern Maroons play one after another *aleke*, and by 12:30 there are very few people left in the tent.

*Friday, 3 July*

Songo and Gazon are sitting in a bus waiting for the morning departure to The Site. After a few minutes, they decide to disembark, commenting that it is not proper for *gaanman*s to have to sit and wait. The women spot their favorite busdriver, who smiles and waves to them to get on. When we join them with the rest of the group, he asks us to transmit a request for their song about the golden horses, and they comply enthusiastically.

A man in a cowboy hat sitting across the aisle from us who's heard what the driver is saying tells us proudly that he works with horses too; he's a saddle maker from New Mexico. A conversation strikes up between him and Djangili, with us as interpreters. He describes how, no matter how many years he's in the trade, he's always learning new tricks to make his saddles better. Djangili latches onto the comment with enthusiasm and remarks that it's the same for a woodcarver. Awagi seconds him, referring to ritual knowledge: no one ever finishes becoming expert at anything, he asserts— there's always something more to be learned, no matter what field of endeavor you're in.

After the groups have unpacked the supplies they've stowed the night before in locked coffers behind the generic structures, the Saramakas put on a spontaneous forest-spirit "play" to honor the three chiefs. Like the similar Eastern Maroon-led offering of last week, this was one of the performative highlights of the Festival. The gates had not yet opened.

The day's activities include a now-familiar mix: music and dance on the main stage, construction-paper patchwork designs, cooking with

> [At St. Louis in 1904], the daily program of the [Filipino] **Negrito** village . . . included: the celebration of marriages, celebrations of annual memorials for deceased relatives, general dances in which all sing, shooting with arrows, making fire and hunting with wild dogs. (Benedict 1983:50)

peanuts, and narrative-stage sessions on dress and ornament, traditions of self-government, and women's lives.

At the Saramakas' afternoon appearance on the main stage, Hélène was looking forward to a special dance in her friend's memory, but it never came; the performers had decided among themselves to handle her request in a different way. After leaving the stage, they called her into the dressing room, showed her where they wanted her to stand, and formed a semi-circle around her, setting a tone that contrasted strongly with the animated performance they had just finished. Each one in turn embraced her and spoke of the need to face life with courage in spite of her sorrow. Then they sang a slow, haunting song in unison, and each embraced her again. Her tears flowed.

Meanwhile, Rich had juggled his responsibilities with other presenters so that, for the first time during the Festival, he would be able to absent himself from the site for two hours at lunch. He's scheduled for a meeting at OAS headquarters with three lawyers from the team that will be representing the Saramakas in their case against the government of Suriname, to be heard next week before the Inter-American Court of Human Rights in San José, Costa Rica. The meeting, run by David Padilla (Assistant Executive Secretary of the Inter-American Commission on Human Rights) is about the logistics of what will happen in San José. Also present are Ambassador Oliver Jackman, distinguished jurist from Barbados, and Elizabeth Houppert, a young lawyer on the staff of the Commission.

After the lunch meeting, Rich suggests they stop by at the Festival, so that they can meet some Saramakas in person and set up a formal meeting with Chief Songo to discuss the case. The highlight of the visit is serendipitous—they arrive at the main stage just as the Saramakas have finished their post-performance presentation to Hélène, and Rich is able to introduce the lawyers in the semi-privacy of the dressing room tent. When he explains that these are the people who will be representing them in the Pokigoon atrocities case, Aduengi exclaims, "But I was there!" and proceeds to recount, with considerable emotion, what he saw at the landing place that day. It had never occurred to Rich that anyone at the Festival might have been an eyewitness, and the unexpectedness of Aduengi's testimony helped the horrors come alive for the lawyers, who had known the chilling details of the case mainly on paper.

After the day's events at The Site, we take our car and drive Aduengi and Songo to a particular suburban Woolworths, some miles away, to buy more aluminum pots. They had been at the Pan-Maroon

Meeting when other Saramakas had bought them on the first shopping trip, and they were eager to have the same model for their various wives. As we enter the large, well-populated store Aduengi remarks with a chuckle that he forgot to change out of his Saramaka clothes; he's wearing a breechcloth, shoulder cape, tassled neckerchief, jaunty golfer's hat, and flip-flops. No one stares visibly or comments. The Festival frame isn't there.

Meanwhile, Djangili had taken the women on a ride in the metro, and they'd had another stroll through the underground shopping area, this time on their own. Street smarts (not unrelated to hunting skills in the rain forest) go a long way in compensating for non-literacy.

At dinner, Songo asks Rich if he would take him out to a drugstore afterwards—he still needs some toothpaste and other personal items. So, they walk the couple of blocks, along raised ramps poised over traffic circles, to the nearest mini-mall. On the way back, a homeless woman mutters good evening and extends a shaky hand holding a plastic cup. After they walk by, Songo asks who she was. Rich explains. Songo says, "Let's go back," and pulls out a dollar for her. "A *gaamá*," he reminds Rich, "must never see a person in need, anywhere, and not help out."

Late evening at the hotel. Samo, a Saramaka brought to the U.S. by missionaries two decades ago and now a housepainter in Maryland, made a formal presentation to Chief Songo: a large carton containing several buckets of Kentucky Fried Chicken and many cans of soft drinks and beer. Songo had Aduengi go from room to room knocking on doors and making the distribution just as if it had been a tapir shot by a hunter on the upper Suriname River.

*Saturday, 4 July*

As we board the bus, Rich once again greets the several Palenqueros whose names he has learned, as well as a couple of the Seminoles and Jamaicans. He suddenly realizes that he'll be leaving the next morning without ever having had (or made) the time for a real conversation with any of them.

The buses took a special round-about route to avoid the streets cordoned off for the upcoming holiday parade. We told the people sitting with us about the high-stepping marching bands and other attractions they could expect to see. But in the end they were kept so busy on the Festival grounds that they never got so much as a peek.

Final cash payments at 9:00 A.M. in the administrative trailer. The presenters' meeting includes special warnings from experienced Smithsonian staff that we should tell the people we're responsible for to be super-careful about professional pickpockets, who would be roaming Festival grounds on this most crowded of all days. (Sibe, the diminutive older Ndjuka woman, had already lost a wad of cash she had stowed in her bra; Ken and Diana had passed the hat at a presenters' meeting to replace it. Sibe appeared at the next day's meeting, tears in her eyes and hands quietly clapping, to express her gratitude.)

Before the gates open for the day, Patricia and Kayanasii make a visit to the long row of white Spot-a-Pots across from the Maroon area. Coming back from these generic outhouses (plastic shell, non-flush hole, hook-and-eye latch), Patricia comments dreamily: "Wouldn't it be neat if we could take them back! Think of having one of those for your very own in Saramaka!"

The Festival guide's disclaimer that "Schedules are subject to change" carries greater weight with each passing day. Today the main stage program, originally slated to begin at 11:00, then changed to 12:00, is starting at 1:00. The Council House schedule has also been cut back to less than half of what's in the program book. The Guiana Maroons are assigned three of the main stage's four hours: Saramaka music and dance introduced by Adiante, Eastern Maroon music and dance introduced by Rich, and Saramaka tale-telling introduced and translated by Sally. The Saramaka women have made a wood fire and are tying *muungá* again. And Aliseti critiques more construction-paper patchwork creations in the Activity Center.

In the middle of the day, a member of the "1st Virginia Regiment" in full eighteenth-century regalia and musket came through the Maroon area with his family after marching in the parade. We explained to the Saramakas that his gun and uniform were similar to those of the soldiers who had fought against their early ancestors, and translated the comparative note to him. He said his name was Bruce Murray and introduced his wife Natalie, and the Saramakas let them take a number

Fig. 14  July 4 on the Mall. Left to right: Ayumbakaa (wearing a hat from the parade), Kayanasii, Patricia, Bruce Murray, Aliseti, Aduengi (holding the musket), Akumayai. *Photo by Natalie Murray*

of pictures. (Unlike almost all the other visitors who took pictures of Saramakas at the Festival, they later sent us prints to forward to Suriname.)

Back at the hotel in the evening, Rich packs his bag for the next morning's trip to Costa Rica. His participation in the Festival had been planned from the beginning with the organizers' knowledge that he would have to slip out a day early to serve as expert witness at the Saramakas' human rights trial. He's more than a little anxious about what's going to happen.

David Padilla from the OAS shows up at the hotel as planned, and Rich brings him to Chief Songo's room where, in Aduengi's presence, they go over the case once more, getting Songo's thoughts about the size and nature of the compensation being requested on behalf of the Saramaka people. It's a quiet, dignified meeting. Everyone is thinking ahead to what will happen in far-off San José. At the end, Songo gives Rich and David a kind of blessing as well as the admonition to be on their guard—he knows who and what they're going to be up against.

Later in the evening, we take almost all the Saramakas out onto the upper level of the Marriott's parking garage to watch the fireworks display across the river near the Washington Monument. We bump into Ian Hancock and exchange some thoughts on the Festival; we've all been so busy with the trivia of daily routine that we've had precious little time to talk.

Ian says that his folks are frequently confronted with people who are blatantly rude. Visitors come up to them and after staring, make remarks about which ones look White and Indian and Negro. The Seminoles, he says, are irritated because they feel that the program organizers are pouring all their energy into the Guianas contingent. Ian

> **Laureen Waukau, a Menominee Indian, told Stan Steiner: "Just recently I realized that I hate whites. When the tourist buses come through and they come in here and stare at me, that's when I hate them. They call me 'Injun.' Like on television. It's a big joke to them. You a 'drunken Injun' they say. . . . I hate it.". . . The tourist who calls an Indian 'Injun' means to insult, but the well-intended tourist on the same bus is no less insulting. Steiner describes an encounter between Waukau and a tourist: "One lady gently touched the young girl's wrist. 'Dear, are you a real Indian?' she asked. 'I hope you don't mind my asking. But you look so American.'" (MacCannell 1992:27–28, citing Evans-Pritchard 1989:97)**

also says he would have liked a blackboard and chalk for his sessions. People assume, he says, that creole languages are broken English (or French) or impoverished dialects. In general, the Seminoles were bothered by having too many Smithsonian volunteers hanging around, especially in their kitchen demonstrations. We told him that we had too few, that there were often none available when we had a scant half hour to go to lunch and needed someone to watch over our "generic structure."

The Saramakas were not terribly impressed with the fireworks. They've seen that sort of thing before in Paramaribo, where the fireworks come direct from the People's Republic.

As Rich says goodnight to Aduengi and Songo, he notices a lineup of partly used mini-bottles of hotel shampoo and body gel on their sink and tells them it's okay to take these home when they leave. Songo says absolutely not, since that would reflect badly. People might say that Saramakas were so poor they had to steal shampoo belonging to the hotel.

*Sunday, 5 July*

A staff person offers to drive Rich to the airport in the morning, and they have a chance to talk for the first time. "We all know you're planning to write a book," she says, "and I've been told to be careful about what I say." But she *does* want to talk. She says that the reason the Festival is so disorganized is that eighty percent of the employees are "on contract" with the Smithsonian from April through July and the permanent staff neither knows them nor really trusts them. There are constant problems in the delegation of authority, with people lower down in the hierarchy not being told what to do till the last second.

As people get off the bus she drives every afternoon between The Site and the hotel, she has begun asking each person she's gotten to know: "What's the dumbest question you were asked today?" The adobe-makers have been telling her about the endless stream of people who want to know: "Is that real dirt?" And the American Indians constantly get asked, "What country are you guys from?" She says they really get frustrated with that one.

There was apparently a big flap—a threatened total walkout—by one or all of the American Indian groups because there's a participant from New Mexico who claims to be Indian but who the others say is not. He was accused (or convicted?) at some time in the past of raping an American Indian woman. And this is his second time at the Festival. She tells other such stories. Some of the New Mexicans, she says, have begun pretending they don't speak English, as a way to avoid talking with visitors. Rich realizes that we've been so wrapped up, twenty-four hours a day, with the Maroons that we've heard almost nothing about the other groups.

Every group, she reports, is filled with its own discontents and political infighting about such issues as who was chosen to participate. She has heard people talking about the dissatisfaction over differential pay, and expresses outrage at the reply she's heard: that the Smithsonian has always done it that way. "Don't you think it's time for them to catch up with post-colonial realities?" she asks.

She says she's heard tremendous prejudice from the New Mexicans against the black Maroons, and resentment against what they see as their privileged status. And the Seminoles, she says, have complained a lot about the Maroons from the Guianas, objecting that they don't wash enough and that they don't cover their bodies. She quotes them as saying, "After all, they're in America. Our people have learned how to dress, so why can't they?" "You'd be amazed to hear the stuff people are saying," she tells Rich, as he thanks her for the ride.

In the airport, he reflects about the politics of race at the Festival, the ways it formed a muted leitmotif running through the whole Maroon visit to Washington—although not a great deal seemed to filter through linguistic barriers to the Alukus, Ndjukas, or Saramakas themselves. From the racist slurs uttered about them in the White House, to the near apotheosis by some members of African American religious groups at the Booko Dei, to the rude questioning about Seminole racial identity, the Maroons were continuously fit into ready-made ideological frames. And how, in late-twentieth century America, could it possibly have been otherwise? From the little we heard, it is clear that the "racial" identity of presenters was an issue of deep concern to some visitors. But, perhaps because it made things go more

> [There were objections by some visitors about] the inappropriate-ness of having non-practitioners of the traditions, (largely white anthropologists), doing the majority of the introductions [at the Booko Dei]. (Bilby and N'Diaye 1992b)

smoothly given the "racially mixed" group of staff, presenters, and volunteers in the Maroon Program, this issue wasn't addressed in public. For better or worse, American racism was one aspect of the Festival experience that did not particularly figure on the Saramakas' or Ndjukas' own list of concerns.

Back on the Mall, Sunday turns out to be the longest day of all. The Guiana Maroons hold a long meeting-*cum*-ceremony before the Festival gates are opened, to express thanks to everyone who had worked so hard to make the Festival happen; the FAF-staff equivalent in the Council House is a little more summary. Adiante has a heavy schedule: almost two hours on the main stage, a session in the Council House, and woodcarving in the Activities Center. Sally moderates a program on "Innovation and Personal Style in Dress" and presents a main-stage program of Saramaka music and dance.

The grand finale in the Maroon area is to be an all-groups medley from 4:00 to 5:00 on the main stage. The penultimate program featured Saramaka folktales, including one about the discovery of Woman, in which the four women displayed considerable comic-theatrical talent as gnarled, unrefined primal creatures waiting to be discovered by Man. Adiante did his best to capture both meaning and flavor in English, no mean task for a native Saramaccan-speaker, and both he and the Saramaka performers were ready for a well-earned break at four o'clock. But the Jamaicans, whose contribution to the finale was scheduled first, were nowhere in sight. Sally took the microphone and filled in with background ethnography about the Maroons, pleas for visitors to thank the Maroons for their performances by buying their crafts in the Museum Shop, and announcements that the grand finale would start in a few moments, trying to hold the audience till the performers showed up. But as the clock ticked on and the Jamaicans were nowhere in sight, she held a mini-consultation with the Saramakas to see if they were game to return to the stage. They were sweaty and

Fig. 15 Saramakas bidding adieu after their tale-telling performance on the main stage. Left to right: Awagi, Patricia, Aliseti, Kayanasii, Akumayai, Djangili, and Aduengi. *Photo courtesy Smithsonian Institution Center for Folklife Programs and Cultural Studies*

tired from their just-completed appearance, but the idea of getting their obligations over with sounded good, and back they went.

Wrapping up to go home proved even more exhausting than the day's performance activities. The first step was to stand in line at the Museum Shop, waiting to straighten out paperwork and get a check for those items that had been sold; this process took two hours for some Saramaka tradition-bearers. Next was more waiting in line, this time at the administration trailer to turn those checks into cash.

Within the Suriname group, the opportunity to sell goods in the U.S. followed lines of established authority. Aliseti, who ranked low in the pecking order, was allowed to bring only a few calabashes, and cleared about $50. Songo and Aduengi sold a total of (if memory serves) $483, with $300 going to Songo and the rest to Aduengi. District Commissioner Libretto brought several large woodcarvings that he had purchased in Suriname and resold them at a tidy profit. And we were told that a chaired professor from a nearby university had, before the group's departure from Suriname, been able to order a carved stool for himself and have it shipped at Smithsonian expense, with no one the wiser.

Then came the job of packing up their area of The Site: dismantling the carvings on the architectural displays, taking down the dishware and textiles they had used to turn their generic structures into culturally marked environments, assembling the paraphernalia they had used for the foodways projects and ongoing demonstrations, folding up all their costumes and musical instruments, taking care of the wooden forest-spirit figure that Aliseti had carried in many of the main-stage performances, and so on. FAF staff told the women they could keep the plastic and enamel dishware that had been bought to decorate their generic structure, and there was much discussion about who would get what.

Then, an extended dispute between Maroons and staff members about who should be responsible for the transportation of the heavy drums and mortars. Festival employees argued that the Smithsonian, having spent so much to provide air travel for the Maroons, had no money left in the budget for excess baggage. The Maroons protested that the drums and mortars had been brought because the Festival organizers had requested them and that they shouldn't have to check them on as their personal baggage. By the time the tradition-bearers decided simply to get their stuff onto a bus at the other side of the Mall and return to the hotel, the issue was still unresolved. At least one Eastern Maroon mortar had been badly cracked at some point in the Festival and had to be left behind; some of the drums had also suffered damage. To our knowledge, no one offered to compensate the owners.

Sunday night: Sally and Awagi realize they had better do something about the things that have been brought back from The Site and deposited—disorganized, unlabeled, and unpacked—in the Festival's ground-level Administration room at the Marriott. They first separate out personal belongings (tape recorders, large numbers of red delicious apples and canned soft drinks, the left-over construction paper which Vivien Chen had offered to Aliseti in recognition of her faithful patchwork service), packed a bunch of it in cartons, tracked down some tape to close them, and put Awagi's name on with a magic marker. Awagi, who had come down with a bad cold and was exhausted, argued that the drums could be left unwrapped; if they got messed up he would know how to fix them back in Suriname. But by the time the drums were loaded onto buses the next morning, they had been neatly wrapped in protective cardboard and securely tied by FAF staffers, including Ken, during a long night devoted to a thousand and one end-of-Festival responsibilities.

Sally got to the dining room near the conclusion of meal service and sat down with a few Maroons; she noticed two of the Saramaka women at the buffet table, but they disappeared without sitting down. She later learned that the women, seeing that no rice was being served, had been loading up plates with meat and vegetables to take back to their room, where they had a supply of *kwáka* (a granola-like version of baked cassava, made by Eastern Maroons, that sometimes substitutes for rice in their meals), when a Marriott worker stopped them. The hotel staff had decided that when Festival participants brought food back to their rooms they took more than when they ate in the dining room. Learning, through a program translator, that taking food to their room wasn't allowed, the women stomped off saying that they wouldn't eat dinner, and besides were going to refuse to perform at the party.

When Sally heard a little later about the incident, she pleaded with a hotel worker (as she had done on several other occasions) to bring a pot of rice from one of the other kitchens in the hotel, and then rushed off to track down the women so they could have something to eat before the beginning of the final pan-Festival party; she had been assigned responsibility for getting the Guiana Maroons to perform. In the end they grudgingly agreed to come back to the dining room for a rice-based meal and to contribute a segment to the evening's entertainment.

People then started gathering for the party. According to the program, Richard Kurin was going to open the festivities at 9:00 by speaking and handing out Certificates of Appreciation to tradition-bearers and presenters; a Saramaka performance was to follow next. At 9:15, the Saramakas weren't there, but neither had there been any opening comments or the presentation of certificates. When the event's organizer asked Sally where the Saramakas were, she said she would check as soon as Kurin began to speak; in the meantime they were all busy packing. "No, but Kurin has decided he doesn't want to go first," she was told, "and we've got to get started right away if we're going to get through the whole program."

A frantic dash upstairs to round up the performers; they were all over the hotel—many in the shower, and none in appropriate dance clothing. The drums were safely locked in Festival headquarters on the first floor, but Sally had fortunately not yet returned the key after her packing session with Awagi. It was as chaotic a preparation as any over the past ten days, but the performers understood the rush and managed to pull themselves together. Joined by the Eastern Maroons, they played *kawina* and the audience was enthusiastic. The Alukus, who didn't have a plane to catch the next morning, stayed for more of the performances, but the Saramakas made an immediate beeline to their rooms to finish packing. The women assembled in one of the rooms to divvy up the four suitcases filled with children's clothing that Hélène had given them as a parting present, asking Sally to serve as an impartial partitioner of the booty into four equal portions.

Earlier in the day Hélène also expressed a wish to give the large banner that had hung at the entrance to the Maroon area to the

Saramakas, but said she didn't know how (to whom) to present it. Sally suggested that offering it to the *gaamá* would be the best way to give it to the group as a whole, and that he would hang it in his official headquarters back in Suriname. Around dinnertime Songo asked to be taken to the woman who had sent the banner, first making sure that he understood exactly which one she was. He was acting coy and kind of mysterious. Sally set up the meeting outside the dining hall and interpreted a thank-you conversation in which compliments flowed effusively. "I only regret that I have nothing to repay this lovely present," he lamented over and over. Even making allowances for formal Saramaka rhetoric, Sally felt as though he was acting funny. At one point he said how dismayed he was that he couldn't communicate all this directly, then remarked about how smiles carry more meaning than words and how wonderful it was to see a smile on the face of a woman as beautiful as she. . . . Reluctantly, he finally accepted that the conversation had come to an end. Walking away, he confided to Sally that he understood that the woman was married, having seen her husband at the dance party, but nonetheless was very taken by her. "I would have liked to ask for her," he said with a wistful smile. The whole incident had a sweet innocence about it.

The next morning, buses took the Suriname delegation to the airport at 7:30.

Fig. 16 Maroons from the Guianas assemble for a group photo. Front center are (left to right) Chiefs Adochini, Gazon, and Songo. *Photo by Roland L. Freeman*

# Afterword

> Why, indeed, as we approach the millennium, is the pub-
> lic folk festival, burdened as it is with discredited social
> and anthropological ideas, grounded in a thoroughly sus-
> pect concept, . . . aggravated by ideological conflict and
> class antagonism, a feature of the cultural landscape at all?
>
> (Cantwell 1992:294–95)

If participating in the Festival was, by turns, exhilarating, exhausting, fun, annoying, eye-opening, frustrating, fascinating, boring, engaging, and alienating, writing about the Festival for publication has been an equally mixed, and wrenching, experience. How could it be otherwise when we are writing about one group of people for whom we have great intellectual respect and personal admiration (of whom Ken only heads the list) engaged in "festivalizing" another group of people for whom we feel not only respect and admiration, but also the kind of solidarity and (in this context) responsibility that builds up over a quarter century of intense involvement as ethnographers?

We were very clear, from the moment that our participation was broached as a possibility, that writing a reflective analysis of the experience would be part of the package, and we never received anything but cooperation from FAF personnel toward that end. Our requests for information were always answered promptly; reports were shared with us courteously; and we were given access to FAF tapes and photo archives for the final checking of details.

At the same time, we were acutely aware, from the git-go, that public critique of the FAF would be touchy indeed. There had been a general lack of critical discourse—attributed by at least one commentator to the dependence on government funding of most potential critics. And those criticisms that were published had triggered inordinately hostile rebuttals. As the 1992 event unfolded and we began to encounter organizational glitches in planning such matters as the hotel meals, the treatment of the chiefs, the disbursement of compensation, and the handling of visa options, we felt ourselves being tagged by some of the FAF staff as trouble-makers. When we articulated intellectual reservations about aspects of the exhibiting frames themselves, we understood from the responses that we were being viewed as uncooperative with the Festival spirit.

The table of contents for this essay does not reflect the order in which its parts took shape. The "diaries" (the edited and expanded texts based on our on-the-spot notes) came first. Most of the "sidebars" were added next, as we broadened our exposure to relevant literature. The opening pages on "exhibiting others" were written several months after our return from Washington, as we sought to situate the event in an anthropological frame that would complement Cantwell's more general contextualization of folklife festivals (1993, which we read in manuscript). The afterword and preface were the final parts to be written, based in part on new materials sent us in the summer of 1993 by the always-cooperative Smithsonian staff. We have worried, throughout the process, about offending sensibilities of colleagues and friends who de-vote themselves unselfishly to something they believe in strongly. Our observations are offered in the hope that those who engage in Festival-making will be able to harness them constructively for the future.

In our experience, the folklorists who work for the FAF act as if bound by a double obligation—to be well-versed in the latest critical theory relating to (re)presentation in festival settings, and at the same time to come down, when all is said and done, on a positive note about the Festival as a whole. It's as if, despite all the problems inherent in the genre and all the practical constraints (lack of funds, insufficient time, etc.), the FAF staff, by means of what Cantwell has mischievously glossed as "magic," comes up with a product they are virtually obli-gated to see as wonderful.

In the aftermath of post-Festival evaluation sessions held by both the Maroon Program staff and the larger FAF staff, organizers Bilby and N'Diaye wrote a formal evaluation (1992a), which they later shared with us. The bulk of it is devoted to "Issues of Presentation and Representation"—in particular, "some of the more problematic aspects of the encounters that took place on the Mall." Given the authorship of these reflections, they deserve careful consideration, as a comple-ment to our own observations.

Ken and Diana begin by recalling the special risks of objectification and of reproducing negative stereotypes "when participants are invited to the festival from societies whose cultures are unfamiliar to the vast majority of festival visitors." And they suggest that the antidote is "dialogue" (achieved through context-sensitive presentations, cultural mediation and interpretation by the presenters, and face-to-face interaction between visitors and participants) designed to "increase cross-cultural understanding and appreciation."

That more such dialogue did not take place "can be attributed," in their view, "largely to . . . the insufficient number of competent interpreters and cultural mediators on site at any given moment" because of budgetary limitations. "Unfortunately," they add, "interpreters were rarely available. . . . [There] were not only too few, but [they] were generally much too busy—often in the role of presenter at the main music and dance tent, in the learning center, or at the narrative stage." The result, as they describe it, was that Maroons often found themselves "surrounded by groups of onlookers with whom they were unable to communicate effectively. Visitors would often attempt to ask them questions; receiving no response, they would then sometimes turn to other visitors and hold speculative conversations among themselves about what was going on."

Ken and Diana go on to recognize that physical aspects of The Site caused distancing, and point in particular to "the generic pre-fab structures . . . [which] powerfully framed everything and everyone inside them . . . heightened by the fact that many of the people so-framed were dressed in ways that would strike visitors as 'colorful' and 'exotic.'" And they mention the similar effect of the white plastic chains, required by fire laws, that defined the foodways area.

They found the presentations on the narrative stage "successful to varying degrees." In general, they felt that this part of the program largely avoided problems of objectification, because of the presence of presenters/interpreters. And they note that the "anxiety and extra work" caused by last-minute changes when "presenters felt that the themes or topics chosen for discussion by the curators were culturally or otherwise inappropriate" could have been circumvented had there been some mechanism for presenters to be consulted at an early stage about the sessions they would be presenting.

They comment that the geographic isolation of most of the groups involved meant that pre-Festival communication was always difficult, and that it would have been very helpful to have a few extra days in Washington before the Festival began, in order to plan out activities, programs, and presentations with the Maroons themselves. Nor was there time allotted in the schedule "for Maroons from different countries to interact and learn systematically about each other's cultures." If that had been possible, "many of the participants might have gone away with an even greater sense of satisfaction."

The report concludes: "Lest the critical tone of these remarks give the wrong impression, we would like to emphasize that we consider the Maroon program in most respects to have been a great success. . . . In making these reservations the focus of our evaluation, we intend merely to suggest a few of the ways in which a festival program that most everyone seems to have found remarkable and exciting (if also challenging and exhausting) might have been rendered yet more rewarding."

Ken and Diana's program evaluation, as well as their separate report on the Booko Dei (prepared for one of its sponsors, the National Museum of American History), includes other upbeat conclusions. There is, for example, a striking passage that illustrates the ways a skilled presenter/translator can facilitate meaningful cross-cultural dialogue—a vignette of the Festival as it's *supposed* to happen:

> On one occasion, Bilby paid a brief visit to an Aluku drummaker who was skillfully putting a new head on his instrument. Onlookers asked many questions about where the craftsman was from and what exactly he was doing, which Bilby translated. [N.B. Bilby had spent several years doing fieldwork with Alukus and wrote his dissertation on their culture.] The drummaker gave several answers, which Bilby in turn translated into English. Then an African American drummer came along and began to ask interesting questions about the techniques everyone was watching, and the personal and social significance of building and repairing drums. This led to other questions from the growing crowd. The Aluku craftsman told Bilby he was enjoying himself, and asked him to stay on awhile longer so that the conversation might continue. A white woman approached and asked whether the man didn't mind people standing around and staring at him as if he were "in a fish bowl." After making sure that his own understanding of the intent of her question was correct, Bilby translated it

for the drummaker, capturing the sense of her "fish bowl" with the term "zoo" (using the French pronunciation)—a concept with which the Aluku man was familiar from his visits to coastal French Guiana. The drummaker smiled, and replied with great dignity that he did not see it that way; but rather, that having all these people from other countries gather around and watch so closely what he was doing gave him *kaakiti* ("strength" or "power"), and made him think about how special the knowledge received from his ancestors was. (Bilby and N'Diaye 1992a:5)

And they conclude their Booko Dei report by citing diverse positive feedback they'd heard from visitors:

that the Booko Dei was inspirational; that the event was an important educational experience; that the dancing and drumming powerfully brought across the message of African survival in the Americas; that it was truly a joyous occasion; that it was "deep"; that the quality of the musical and dance performances was excellent and that people who attended felt blessed to have the opportunity to meet and interact with members of the Maroon community. (Bilby and N'Diaye 1992b)

Along with these evaluations, we were also sent copies of the seven letters or postcards from Maroon participants that had been received by FAF staff over the year since the Festival took place. Three of the Jamaicans sent letters, all handwritten on lined paper, expressing warm thanks for the Festival and the hope that they might be invited back. Johannes Toyo sent a postcard from Suriname saying he had had a very nice time. André Pakosie, the Dutch-based Ndjuka who had read a statement at the Maroon People's Meeting, expressed appreciation for that event and the hope that there would be a follow-up. District Commissioner Libretto wrote Richard Kurin to thank the FAF on behalf of the *gaanman*s and other Suriname participants. And finally Mayor Abienso sent Diana Parker (under a letterhead with three telephone numbers, a fax number, and the official seal of Maripasoula) a typed letter in the Aluku language, quite possibly the only one emanating from his office over the course of the entire year that was not in French—he must have remembered her opening greetings in nineteen languages.

On the basis of our own experience, the critical points made in the various FAF self-evaluations seem largely on target. At the same time we wonder whether their more positive conclusions don't bear closer scrutiny. Mightn't one suggest, for example, that the problematics of representation are not settled simply by a determination of whether or not the Aluku drummaker thinks he's in a zoo[19] (or whether or not the *gaanman*s felt demeaned by being put on display)? Or that the desire of participants to replay the experience may not provide the litmus test for the acceptability of the undertaking? Or that the prestige accruing to participants once they get back home may fail to justify what they went through?

During the late-nineteenth century, many of the individuals and groups who were exhibited in Europe and the U.S. expressed heartfelt gratitude and the genuine wish to return for another show. Indeed, many of them did return, some year after year and fair after fair. The pygmy Ota Benga apparently begged to be brought back to the U.S., where he had been a prime exhibit at the St. Louis Fair; eventually his wish was fulfilled, and he was exhibited in the monkey cage of the Bronx Zoo. And the other pygmies who danced with him on the Plaza St. Louis and suffered countless indignities still spread tales among their compatriots of how wonderful their trip had been (Bradford and Blume 1992:141, 149, pass.).

And then there's the case of Saartjie Baartman, "The Hottentot Venus," who "won her fame as a sexual object" because Europeans fit her steatopygous body-shape into their exotic-erotic fantasies. Put on view in early nineteenth-century England and France, she exhibited her charms upon command: "on being ordered by her keeper, she came out . . . and [was] ordered to move backwards and forwards and come out and go into her cage." When "interrogated in Dutch before a court" that was trying to protect her from exploitation, she "insisted that she was not under restraint and understood perfectly well that she had been guaranteed half the profits. The show went on" (Gould 1985:293-94, 296, pass.). We have strong memories, as students in Paris in 1963, of standing before a tall museum case holding a life-like naked cast of "La Vénus Hottentot(te)" in the Musée de l'Homme (for a photo, see S. Price 1988:23). And today in that august museum's storage facilities, visiting scientists can still examine, in a jar prepared in 1815 by "France's greatest anatomist" Georges Cuvier, Saartjie Baartman's dissected genitalia.

# Notes

1. The bibliographies in R. and S. Price 1991 and 1992 provide selected references to this work; see also R. Price 1995, R. and S. Price 1994, 1995a, 1995b. Although many funding agencies have contributed to our past research in these areas, we are particularly indebted to the National Endowment for the Humanities for major grants supporting our work on the arts (1979–81) and oral literature (1985–88), and to the National Science Foundation for work on oral history (1976–78).

2. These examples of fifteenth- and sixteenth-century Europeans exhibiting live others are nearly random, chosen from a much longer list. For a particularly fine review and bibliography, see Mason n.d.

3. In a recent book on the 1893 Chicago fair, Robert Muccigrosso claims, *pace* "recent critics" (presumably such as Rydell), that the arrangement of foreign villages on the Midway did not demonstrate "racial and ethnic biases . . . [or] proclaim the superiority of white, Eurocentric culture" (1993:164). Other than quoting Frederick Douglass's angry comment about the Dahomey Village— "African savages brought here to act the monkey" (1993:146)—his book glosses quickly over the extensive non-Western exhibits (1993:164–65) and reads more like a celebration of the exposition than a historical analysis of it.

4. Monsanto points out that these claims of diversity suffered from hyperbole, but that, "following the lead of the American Museum freakshow [which preceded the Congress], Barnum hired Asian immigrants and African Americans to play the roles of the ethnic groups he could not recruit" (ibid.).

5. Such exhibitions continued, without scientific support, even after anthropologists had abandoned the scientific racism that had supported their earlier incarnations. In 1927, the Ringling Brothers & Barnum & Bailey Circus exhibited "Cliko, the African bushman," in 1930 "a tribe of genuine Ubangi savages . . . [with] mouths and lips as large as those of full-grown crocodiles," and in 1933 a pair of "giraffe-necked" Burmese women (Monsanto 1992:29).

6. Robert Cantwell's ambitious *Ethnomimesis* attempts to situate the FAF historically within the emergence of modernity, relating the seventeenth- and eighteenth-century enclosures in England, "and the landscape gardens that followed upon them . . . [to] the Quincy Markets, the Harbor Places [which are called "festival markets" by their developers], the historical districts, tourist attractions, theme parks, suburban tracts, shopping malls, and, indeed, to the folk revivals and folk festivals of our own day" (1993:44).

7. At the behest of the Smithsonian's Office of Folklife Programs, Robert Cantwell made a massive compilation of interviews, essays, reports, and

previously-published articles about the FAF, including the detailed musings of the Festival's founder, Ralph Rinzler, regarding its origins (Cantwell 1988). Most of the newspaper clippings that we quote from past Festivals are taken from this unpublished compilation, which Cantwell kindly shared with us. The document is also available at the Smithsonian's Center for Folklife Programs and Cultural Studies.

8. This is a looseleaf binder containing background about the FAF, the Maroon Program, Schedules, Names of Staff, Site Maps, and the 1992 Presenter's Guide.

9. Bauman and Sawin write:

> The ideological foundation of contemporary American folklife festivals is essentially a kind of liberal pluralism. Folk festivals promulgate a symbolically constructed image of the popular foundations of American national culture by traditionalizing, valorizing, and legitimating selected aspects of vernacular culture drawn from the diverse ethnic, regional, and occupational groups that are seen to make up American society. Folk culture is variously counterpoised against elite, mass, or official culture as embodying values and social relations that are a necessary, natural, and valuable part of human existence, worthy of preservation and encouragement. (1991:289)

10. In our later reading, we found that this defensiveness sometimes assumes near-legendary proportions. The team of Indiana University folklorists who wrote an ethnography of the 1987 FAF, though having designed the research in close collaboration with the director of the Smithsonian's Office of Folklife Programs, were viewed by various staff members "with suspicion and hostility," in extreme cases being addressed as "carpetbaggers" or being seen as "spies" (Bauman et al. 1992:9–13). And the rather mild reflections of another commentator on the Festival were greeted by a blistering riposte by a senior Smithsonian folklorist (Seitel 1991). For additional examples and discussion, see Cantwell 1993.

11. The central portion of this essay is written in the form of a diary. In fact, once we arrived in Washington, we had all too little time to write, though we did our best to keep running notes. The incidents we report are all "true," but exactly when they happened was not always clear from our notes and we have reconstructed (as much as a year later in a few cases) to the best of our memories. Quotes are based on notes we jotted down at the time, though we have since checked as many of them as possible against FAF audio-visual documentation, which the staff kindly shared with us later. Note also that unlike previous Festival commentators (e.g., Robert Cantwell and the team led by Richard Bauman), we were working full-time for the Festival itself, putting in eighteen-hour days, not as ethnographers but as "presenters" and hosts for

the Saramakas (who needed more attention than many festival troupes because they didn't speak English). We had almost no time during our stay in Washington to interview non-Maroons, to reflect analytically about our experience, or for that matter to visit other parts of the Mall and see the rest of the Festival.

12. In commenting on this manuscript, Ken Bilby reported that in his experience Alukus (and at least some Ndjukas) cook cassava on large round griddles as well.

13. Adiante Franszoon is a Saramaka who came back to the U.S. with us in 1968 and stayed on, earning his living in part as a woodcarver.

14. We excerpt this series of greetings from the version that appeared in print at the front of the 1992 Participant Handbook.

15. In commenting on this passage, Ken Bilby suggested that this participant's discomfort was probably "a simple case of shyness and sudden stage fright . . . [about] speaking in public," and described how she had returned as a participant to the FAF the following year, contributing enthusiastically to narrative sessions, including several on herbal medicine.

16. We would like to stress that in addition to our intense ongoing interactions with Ken Bilby, Diana N'Diaye, and the other Smithsonian staffers directly involved in the Maroon Program, we crossed paths informally, on something like an every-other-day basis, with more senior Smithsonian scholars—in particular, Peter Seitel, Richard Kurin, and James Early—who sometimes strolled The Site and sat in on (or even participated in) sessions. Often, we chatted briefly, with one of them asking how our work was going, what our impressions were thus far. We are very grateful for their collegial courtesy throughout the Festival, even as they understood from what we said that we would someday be writing about it from a perspective rather different from their own.

17. For a discussion of human rights violations in 1980s Suriname, and the related 1992 court hearings in Costa Rica, see R. Price 1995.

18. We were later told that President Bush was taking off from his heliopad and that special security was in effect.

19. In commenting on this passage, Bilby expressed concern that we might not be communicating sufficiently the sophistication of the drummaker and his understanding of the representational issues in question. The drummaker, he pointed out,

> didn't feel like an object—or otherwise demeaned—at that moment because he was actively and voluntarily engaged in a meaningful conversation with other individuals, several of whom had reasonable questions, and at least some of whom expressed real interest and admiration for his skills. . . . (That he already knew me, his interpreter, and probably trusted

me, no doubt helped.) Nor did the people looking on—at least those who were talking with him—treat him like an object. His response to the woman's question was calm, measured, and dignified. He was well aware of the implications of the question (as many other Alukus in the same situation, I think, would be, given the way they often talk about French *tuwisi*—tourists—who sometimes treat them like objects, "primitives," etc., in their own territory). And he was quite capable of discussing the implications further (as he and I did a bit later). It was the woman who seemed taken aback by his answer; and she didn't pursue the line of questioning any further. (personal communication, 8 March 1994)

# References

Altick, Richard D. 1978. *The Shows of London*. Cambridge, Mass.: Harvard University Press.

Bauman, Richard, and Patricia Sawin. 1991. The Politics of Participation in Folklife Festivals, in Ivan Karp and Steven D. Lavine, eds., *Exhibiting Cultures: The Poetics and Politics of Museum Display*. Washington, D.C.: Smithsonian Institution Press, pp. 288–314.

Bauman, Richard, Patricia Sawin, and Inta Gale Carpenter. 1992. *Reflections on the Folklife Festival: An Ethnography of Participant Experience*. Bloomington, Ind.: Special Publications of the Folklore Institute.

Berger, John. 1991 [1980]. *About Looking*. New York: Vintage.

Benedict, Burton. 1983. *The Anthropology of World's Fairs: San Francisco's Panama Pacific International Exposition of 1915*. Berkeley, Cal.: Scolar Press.

Bilby, Kenneth, and Diana Baird N'Diaye. 1992a. Maroon Program Staff Evaluation. Unpublished ms. Washington, D.C.: Smithsonian Center for Folklife and Cultural Studies, September.

———. 1992b. Report on Booko Dei Event. Unpublished ms. Washington, D.C.: Smithsonian Center for Folklife and Cultural Studies, September 14.

Bonaparte, Prince Roland. 1884. *Les habitants de Suriname. Notes recueillies à l'exposition coloniale d'Amsterdam en 1883*. Paris: A. Quantin.

Boon, James A. 1991. Why Museums Make Me Sad, in Ivan Karp and Steven D. Lavine, eds., *Exhibiting Cultures: The Poetics and Politics of Museum Display*. Washington, D.C.: Smithsonian Institution Press, pp. 255–77.

Bradford, Phillips Verner, and Harvey Blume. 1992. *Ota Benga: The Pygmy in the Zoo*. New York: St. Martin's Press.

Buck, George N. 1973. Letter to the Editor. *Washington Post*, July 15. [cited in Cantwell 1988:xviii–xix]

Cantwell, Robert. 1988. A Folkways Anthology: Voices from the Festival of American Folklife. Unpublished ms. Washington, D.C.: Smithsonian Institution, Office of Folklife Programs. [on deposit at the Center for Folklife Programs and Cultural Studies, Smithsonian Institution]

———. 1991. Conjuring Culture: Ideology and Magic in the Festival of American Folklore. *Journal of American Folklore* 104:148–63.

———. 1992. Feasts of Unnaming: Folk Festivals and the Representation of Folklife, in Robert Baron and Nicholas R. Spitzer, eds., *Public Folklore*. Washington, D.C.: Smithsonian Institution Press, pp. 263–305.

———. 1993. *Ethnomimesis: Folklife and the Representation of Culture*. Chapel Hill: University of North Carolina Press.

Clifford, James. 1986. Introduction: Partial Truths, in James Clifford and

George E. Marcus, eds., *Writing Culture: The Poetics and Politics of Ethnography*. Berkeley: University of California Press, pp. 1–26.

Collomb, Gérard. 1992a. *Kaliña*. Exhibition brochure for "Kaliña, des Amérindiens de Guyane à Paris en 1892." Musée des Arts et Traditions Populaires, Paris.

———. 1992b. *Kaliña, des Amérindiens à Paris*. Paris: Créaphis.

Corbey, Raymond. 1993. Ethnographic Showcases, 1870–1930. *Cultural Anthropology* 8:338–69.

Evans-Pritchard, Dierdre. 1989. How "They" See "Us": Native American Images of Tourists. *Annals of Tourism Research* 16:89–105.

Faber, Paul, and Steven Wachlin. 1990. Mensen te kijk. *Spiegel Historiael* 25:2–6.

Givens, Shelby M. 1992. The Walk That Wasn't Pedestrian. *Washington Post*, July 12, C8.

Gould, Stephen Jay. 1985. *The Flamingo's Smile: Reflections in Natural History*. New York: W. W. Norton.

Hinsley, Curtis M. 1991. The World as Marketplace: Commodification of the Exotic at the World's Columbian Exposition, Chicago, 1893, in Ivan Karp and Steven D. Lavine, eds., *Exhibiting Cultures: The Poetics and Politics of Museum Display*. Washington, D.C.: Smithsonian Institution Press, pp. 344–65.

Karp, Ivan. 1991. Festivals, in Ivan Karp and Steven D. Lavine, eds., *Exhibiting Cultures: The Poetics and Politics of Museum Display*. Washington, D.C.: Smithsonian Institution Press, pp. 279–87.

Kirshenblatt-Gimblett, Barbara. 1991. Objects of Ethnography, in Ivan Karp and Steven D. Lavine, eds., *Exhibiting Cultures: The Poetics and Politics of Museum Display*. Washington, D.C.: Smithsonian Institution Press, pp. 386–443.

———. 1992 [1988]. Mistaken Dichotomies, in Robert Baron and Nicholas R. Spitzer, eds., *Public Folklore*. Washington, D.C.: Smithsonian Institution Press, pp. 29–48.

Kurin, Richard. 1989. Why We Do the Festival, in Frank Proschan, ed., Smithsonian Festival of American Folklife *Program Book*. Washington, D.C.: Smithsonian Institution, pp. 8–21.

———. 1991. The Festival of American Folklife: Building on Tradition, in Peter Seitel, ed., Smithsonian Festival of American Folklife *Program Book*. Washington, D.C.: Smithsonian Institution, pp. 7–20.

———. 1992. Festival of American Folklife: Not Just a Festival, in Peter Seitel, ed., Smithsonian Festival of American Folklife *Program Book*. Washington, D.C.: Smithsonian Institution, pp. 7–11, 13–14.

Levine, Lawrence W. 1988. *Highbrow/Lowbrow: The Emergence of Cultural Hierarchy in America*. Cambridge, Mass.: Harvard University Press.

MacCannell, Dean. 1992. *Empty Meeting Grounds: The Tourist Papers*. London: Routledge.

Mason, Peter. n.d. *Infelicities: Representations of the Exotic.* Unpublished ms.

McGill, Douglas C. 1984. Center Devoted to African Art Opens. *New York Times.* 18 September, C17.

Mitchell, Timothy. 1992. Orientalism and the Exhibitionary Order, in Nicholas B. Dirks, ed., *Colonialism and Culture.* Ann Arbor: University of Michigan Press, pp. 289–317.

Monsanto, Anthony, Jr. 1992. The Living Proof: The Barnum and Bailey Circus and the Reification of Racial Categories, 1884–1896. Unpublished ms. Religion Department, Princeton University.

Muccigrosso, Robert. 1993. *Celebrating the New World: Chicago's Columbian Exposition of 1893.* Chicago: Ivan R. Dee.

O'Brien, Tom. 1970. Country Folk and the City, *Washington Post,* July 3. [cited in Cantwell 1988:v–vi]

Parker, Diana. 1993. The Festival of American Folklife: Doing More with Less, in Peter Seitel, ed., Smithsonian Festival of American Folklife *Program Book.* Washington, D.C.: Smithsonian Institution, pp. 15–16.

Prakash, Gyan. 1992. Science "Gone Native" in Colonial India. *Representations* 40 (Fall):153–78.

Price, Richard. 1983. *First-Time: The Historical Vision of an Afro-American People.* Baltimore: Johns Hopkins University Press.

——— . 1995. Executing Ethnicity: The Killings in Suriname, in Richard Price and Michel-Rolph Trouillot, eds., *Class, Ethnicity, and Ideology in the Caribbean.*

Price, Richard, and Sally Price. 1991. *Two Evenings in Saramaka.* Chicago: University of Chicago Press.

——— . 1992. *Equatoria.* New York: Routledge.

——— . 1994. Ethnicity in a Museum Case: France's Show-Window in the Americas. *Museum Anthropology* 18, no. 2: 3–15.

——— . 1995a. Executing Culture: Musée, Museo, Museum. *American Anthropologist* 97.

——— . 1995b. Museums, Ethnicity, and Nation-Building: Reflections from the French Caribbean, in Geert Banck, Michiel Baud, and Gert Oostindie, eds., *Looking Forward: Ethnicity and Social Structure in Afro-America.*

Price, Sally. 1988. Arts *primitifs,* regards *civilisés. Gradhiva* 4:19–27.

——— . 1989. *Primitive Art in Civilized Places.* Chicago: University of Chicago Press.

*Reminiscences of the Colonial and Indian Exhibition.* 1886. London: William Clowes.

Rinzler, Ralph. 1976. A Festival to Cherish Our Differences, in *1976 Festival of American Folklife [Program Book].* Washington, D.C.: Smithsonian Institution, p. 7.

Rinzler, Ralph, and Peter Seitel. 1977. Cajun Fiddles, Hindustani *veenas* and Dulcimers. *Smithsonian Magazine* 8, no. 7:142–51.

Rydell, Robert W. 1984. *All the World's a Fair: Visions of Empire at American International Expositions, 1876–1916*. Chicago: University of Chicago Press.

Sawin, Patricia E. 1988. The 1987 Smithsonian Festival of American Folklife: An Ethnography of Participant Experience. Unpublished ms. Folklore Institute, Indiana University Bloomington. [excerpts in Cantwell 1988:732–50]

Seitel, Peter. 1991. Magic, Knowledge, and Irony in Scholarly Exchange: A Comment on Robert Cantwell's Observations on the Festival of American Folklife. *Journal of American Folklore* 104:495–96.

Siporin, Steve. 1992. Public Folklore: A Bibliographic Introduction, in Robert Baron and Nicholas R. Spitzer, eds., *Public Folklore*. Washington, D.C.: Smithsonian Institution Press, pp. 339–70.

Smithsonian Opens Annual Festival to Help Preserve America's Vanishing Folk Culture. 1970. *New York Times*, July 2. [cited in Cantwell 1988:v]

Stanton, Gary. 1992. Review of 1991 Festival of American Folklife. *Journal of American Folklore* 105:235–37.

Stocking, George W., Jr. 1987. *Victorian Anthropology*. New York: The Free Press.

———. 1992. *The Ethnographer's Magic and Other Essays in the History of Anthropology*. Madison: University of Wisconsin Press.

Weintraub, Boris. 1976. Will There Be a Folklife Festival in '77? *Washington Star*, September 12. [cited in Cantwell 1988:xxv–xxvii]